WOMEN IN CUBA:
Twenty Years Later

WOMEN IN CUBA:
Twenty Years Later

by

MARGARET RANDALL

with photographs by

JUDY JANDA

SMYRNA PRESS
NEW YORK, N.Y.

Cover: Judy Janda

Copyright © 1981
by
Margaret Randall

Library of Congress Catalog No. 80-54055

ISBN 0-918266-14-9 (softcover)
ISBN 0-918266-15-7 (hardcover)

SMYRNA PRESS
Box 1803-GPO
Brooklyn, NY 11202

*This book is for Celia Sánchez
and Haydée Santamaría, in memorium*

This book is for my daughter, Ximena

Contents

INTRODUCTION
Michelle Russell 9

AUTHOR'S INTRODUCTION
Socialism and Feminism Need Each Other 13

CHAPTER ONE
The Struggle Against Sexism 21

CHAPTER TWO
Peasant Women in a Changing Society 49

CHAPTER THREE
Woman As Mother: The Right To Free and Complete
Childbearing Attention 67

CHAPTER FOUR
Development of the Family 85

CHAPTER FIVE
To Create Ourselves: Women in Art 107

CHAPTER SIX
The Federation of Cuban Women: The Role of
a Woman's Organization in the Revolutionary Process 123

APPENDIXES
I Thesis Three 137
II "I'll Cook If I Have To" 149
III The Working Woman Maternity Law 152
IV Regulations of Law 1263 159

BIBLIOGRAPHY 163

PHOTOGRAPHS

Introduction

This book is being published in a period when a new wave of Cuban immigrants are being boat-lifted to the U.S. Many are women with children, coming to join husbands, brothers, or others who have sent for them from places such as Miami, Tampa, and Union City. There, they will add themselves to the ever-growing groups of marginal laborers who barely subsist at the bottom of the great American melting pot. They are coming at a time of economic crisis, right-wing reaction, and renewed aggression against Third World nations and peoples in the U.S. Their rude awakening on these shores will consist of realizing that they have not left scarcity, underdevelopment, or social schizophrenia behind. What those women are leaving behind is chronicled in the following pages.

In order for North Americans to grasp fully the significance of the information contained here, a substantial imaginative leap is required. In the U.S. the wrenching social process of women attaining full equality is carried on primarily by those desperately trying to free themselves from the regressive mores and structural irrationalities of a dying culture through patchwork social and economic reforms applied to the corpus of the crumbling old order. Under these conditions, even our fundamental human right to control our own reproductive capacities is in question and comes under constant attack from both official and ad hoc sources in society. In Cuba, the woman's struggle is going on from the opposite end of the social process. There, state power has already been seized from bourgeois capitalist interests. Thus, the social revolution of a society newly mobilized and deliberately reconstructing itself from the ground up according to politically democratic and economically socialist principles is the context informing the course of women's development and liberation. In this process, inequities considered chronic in the U.S. have been eliminated in Cuba over the last twenty years. Whether one looks at such indicators as women's incorporation into the work force, the extent of direct union, shop floor, and community participation in decisionmaking, the division of labor in the home, the security of guaranteed medical care and education from the cradle to the grave, or the general betterment of those worst off in pre-revolutionary times, it becomes clear that at least the material and ideological bases have been laid in Cuba for women to pursue their full capacities as human beings.

To give guidance to this quest, women not only have each other, but the Federation of Cuban Women (FMC). Just imagine, for example, that all the women in the U.S. belonged to a single organization and that it did things such as take its own census of our needs. Imagine that the questions on that census included the following: What changes would you make in the education your children are getting? What work would you like to do? What hours of the day do you need child care? What makes you angriest in a typical day? What activities make you feel most productive? And then, imagine that this organization tabulates the results and takes responsibility for solving these problems and structuring ways that we can continue the process on our own. And imagine that this is just one facet of this national organization's work. Then you will begin to have an idea of the Cuban context.

Beyond this, whole new ways of thinking, seeing, and being are demanded to take advantage of the new opportunities the revolution has initiated. Twenty-two years ago, Cuba was a peasant society, saddled with a one-crop economy under U.S. imperial domination. For women, this meant that they would spend impoverished, male-dominated lives as childbearers, field workers, maids, or whores. Their consciousness would be shaped wholly by those circumstances. In the new society, all that had to be changed. Everyone had to begin again. This produces a profoundly transformative situation which requires "that you pull yourself up by your own hair, turn yourself inside out, and see the whole world through fresh eyes." Every day. Young and old alike. Women and men together. In Cuban terms, Miguel Barnet's poem, "Revolution," summarizes the feeling.

When the revolution came
multitudes entered my house
They seemed to be going through drawers,
closets, changing the sewing basket around

That old silence was no more
and my grandmother stopped weaving memories
stopped speaking
stopped singing

Hopeful I saw, I had to see,
how the light came into that room
when my mother opened the windows
for the first time.

Some become mute under the impact of such an upheaval. Some
rejoice. Some cling desperately to tokens of their old lives. Some
leave. All change as they struggle to follow their own minds
and stay together as a people stepping into the future.

Margaret Randall's survey of Cuba's present-day realities
and her understanding of the developmental road women have
been traveling since the revolution reinforce, above all, the conviction that the simultaneous struggle for bread and roses is the
most demanding and potentially explosive process to which any
society can be wedded. It reminds me, as a North American and
movement activist, how much we have to do and how far we
have to go. It gives me, in no small measure, the strength to
continue.

MICHELE GIBBS RUSSELL
Grenada, West Indies

AUTHOR'S INTRODUCTION

Socialism and Feminism
Need Each Other

*The Revolution gave human beings back their dignity;
it didn't give it to man because I don't think the word* man *includes women. I don't agree that when one is going to talk about
human beings one should say "man." I don't think men would
agree that our saying* woman *when we mean men and women
really includes men.*

> Haydée Santamaría, heroine of Moncada,
> member of the Central Committee of the
> Communist Party of Cuba, member of the
> Council of State, and director of the Casa
> de las Américas.
> *Granma,* 1979.

My working interest in Cuban women began in 1969 when
I came to live and work on the island. At the Book Institute,
where I was first a member of the writing collective at Ambito
(a special projects publishing venture) and later a member of the
Social Sciences Division, I submitted a proposal to do a study
of women in the revolutionary process. It was accepted, and,
for the following two years, a small group (myself, a photo-
grapher, and one or two others) received economic and intellectual support to carry through the project.

We traveled all over the country — by plane, bus, jeep, and
sometimes on horseback. We interviewed women in the rural

13

areas, in factories, and schools. We learned what life had been like for Cuban women before 1959, what changes the revolution brought, and what contradictions remained. The result of that experience was *Cuban Women Now*. Ten years have passed. The Cuban revolution is twice as old. These years have seen a deepening in the process of women's liberation. But the term "women's liberation" — in its means, if not always in its end — may evoke something very different for women in Cuba than for women in the United States.

In August 1978 I was invited to participate in a workshop called "Does Socialism Liberate Women?" at the Fourth Berkshire Conference on Women's History held at Mt. Holyoke College. It seemed a good opportunity to return to and travel in the United States, after an absence of seventeen years, and the extraordinary network (mostly women) we know exists throughout the country quickly produced lecture invitations at seventy universities. This became an opening for sharing the new development in the lives of Cuban women.

I spoke at large state educational institutions such as the University of Wisconsin-Milwaukee, the University of Washington, the State University of New York-Buffffalo, and Colorado State; ruling class schools such as Yale, Wellesley, Pomona, and Sarah Lawrence; community colleges such as Los Medanos in northern California; inner city institutions such as Temple in Philadelphia; and working class schools such as York in Jamaica, Queens. Forty students took a mini-course I gave at Oberlin. At Boston University, there was a wildcat maintenance workers' strike, and, to avoid crossing the picket line, I spoke at a local disco ballroom offered in solidarity for the occasion.

What I had to say about Cuban women, the experience I would bring to these multiple audiences, was challenged, discussed, and enriched by people (again, mostly women) from a variety of backgrounds and social conditions. The well-educated daughters and sons of the ruling class had a wide range of theoretical questions. Minority and working students wanted to know if it was true that there is no longer any unemployment in Cuba. My Oberlin students wrote papers about aspects of the Cuban female experience as it related to their lives. A young black woman in a California community college asked, "Is Cuba still a communist country?" I finished the tour feeling I'd learned as much or more than I'd offered.

Even from a distance, the American women's movement was always central to my life, part of me. But as I traveled from state to state, rediscovering my country and my people, the full force of the movement, as well as the contradictions facing different groups of American women, gripped me and taught me a great deal. The peculiarities of a highly developed class society has produced a women's movement which has forever made some freer while failing others, propelled some women away from compromising alliances with men while leading others to reject males on totally ahistoric principles. A few have been pushed to search seriously for the necessary links between feminism and the scientific laws of society, while others proudly proclaim victories in such panaceas as the apparent control of media designed to file them away in an exploitative system.

In a midwestern state, an articulate thirty-five-year-old single mother and student told me, "The women's movement made me real angry and then didn't come through. . . ." She became a charismatic Christian! In San Francisco, I spent a day looking hard at the wonderful murals, painted largely by women, which are one product of this new collective strength. I was moved, listening to Puerto Rican revolutionary doctor Helen Rodriguez and lesbian poet Adrienne Rich join forces to speak against sterilization abuse, and finding that, in Tempe, Arizona and Oberlin, Ohio, two women Latin Americanists are searching out and translating Latin American female poets often ignored in their own countries.

Copying the texts of subway and bus ads one day in New York City, I noted the following:

> It's Lark Light! It's Lark Light time: a moment ago women's rights! Male chauvinism! Suddenly . . . a warming smile. A light time . . . and a Lark. New Lark Lights. Satisfaction. Flavor and low tar through the exclusive Charcolite filter. Light up. It's the Lark Light time.

The sophisticated Virginia Slim image remains: the woman who tells you, in her sultry put-on, "You've come a long way, baby, and now you've got your very own cigarette!" Lark aims its message at the woman who has had her flirtation with "liberation" and is coming up for air on the far side of a twisted concept. The image accompanying the text is of the slighter half of "the perfect couple" gazing up into her strong man's eyes as he bends to light her cigarette. The threat is clear. So is the system's cooptation of a dangerous presence.

The distorted female image in the plastic culture of TV prize shows such as *The Newlywed Game, Family Feud*, and *Blind Date*, cult movies such as the *Rocky Horror Show*, and innumerable popular song lyrics, sweeps the nation. Against them has surfaced an extremely vibrant women's culture: music, poetry, and theater — whose consciousness is shared with and assimilated by not a few men. Among performers who get away from sexist stereotypes are Sweet Honey in the Rock, Cris Williamson, Meg Christian, Holly Near, The Deadly Nightshade, The Izquierda Ensemble, and Bread and Roses.

The fact is that the liberation of women is neither fad nor illusion but a necessary next step on the historical agenda. In spite of that which would coopt us by passing off manipulation as culture, in spite of media maneuvers and well-meant or evil-intentioned deadends, women all over the world are coming to a consciousness which can ultimately develop and partake of the total human dream: freedom for all beings. I left the United States, after this trip, with an absolute conviction — *socialism and feminism need each other!*

The essays which follow are based on the lectures I gave in the United States in 1978, with the inclusion of additional statistical information and updated material gathered since my return to Cuba. The essays have been written in a form which gives a comprehensive view of Cuban women after twenty years of revolution. The most important revisions seek to deal with the questions, concerns, ideas, and challenges that followed my lectures in formal question-and-answer periods as well as in numerous informal discussions. Therefore, although I take sole responsibility for the limitations in these essays, I thank my audiences and students for helping me to clarify the focus and thrust of this work. I especially wish to single out some women whose thought, work, and lives have been of particular inspiration to me: Joan Kelly-Gadol, Marian McDonald, Blanche

Cook, Clare Coss, Marilyn Young, Jane Norling, Helen Rodríguez, and my mother, Elinor Randall. Making a book is a
complex process that doesn't end with the writing. My editors,
Dan Georgakas and Judy Janda, deserve credit for much of the
coherence and final presentation of this one. Their creativity,
coupled with thoroughness, is an example I learn from. The
photo section, also by Judy Janda, is the product of another
wonderful work relationship. The fact that my own interest in
photography began while working with Judy attests to the depth
of that experience.

Different as the social conditions and cultures are, there is
a dialectic between the Cuban and American women's struggles
to move forward that sometimes translates into a unique and
moving exchange. Barnard College's Women's Center holds a
yearly auction to raise money for its abortion fund. Last year,
a Barnard alumni carefully copied and bound both the Spanish
original and my English translation of a Cuban woman's poem
about her struggle to be free. To be free in a society where a
great part of freedom has been won; where abortion, for one
thing, is no longer a problem, but where sexism remains to
challenge progress. The poem was purchased for twenty-five dol-
lars by the director of the Women's Center, and then donated to
the Center itself; so the money went to the abortion fund and
the poem became a part of the Center's collection. The day I
spoke at Barnard, I was told this story and saw the manuscript.
That night, I wrote to Milagros González, poet and policewoman
on Cuba's Isle of Youth, who, in turn, was moved to discover
her words had served as a stimulus to American women. As a
way of introducing the new Cuban woman and her struggles,
here is the poem:

FIRST DIALOGUE

(With our comrades, who daily...)

> *In that way, put an end to the*
> *old non-communist psychology.*
>
> V. I. Lenin
> (On women's role in society,
> from Clara Zetkin's notebooks)

Here comes my secular skirt again
    and Anguish circles my throat.
These breasts that calmed my daughters' cries
move together, rise, stand up
and strike for the milk of life.

Then I blame myself—old habit—
for my white hands, the head scarves, lipstick, purse,
those nine months dawning,
and fail to understand the root,
                the seed,
                the flower.

Where are you: manspirit of my time,
every afternoon home from work
become exactly that fountain of rude stares
        reproaching me the quick lunch,
        pile of unwashed clothes,
        handkerchiefs not perfectly ironed.
        This daily existence.

So often I see you
red card proud in the pocket of your shirt,
your honors,
your medals,
your gun,
your word: humble *Homeland or Death* of every day
breaking between your hands
where callouses, shovels, papers, all of you move on
        without reproach,
        without protest,
        without a word.

The draining fear comes over me when I meet your wonder
at the rag I hand you
to help dismiss the dust:
that weariness, you don't know how, the newspaper, so tired,
that meeting or what's worse sometimes:
it's just not what you've got planned for today.

Then I remind you of Luis, Pedro, Juan,
the guy across the street
or next door. Nothing.
You're not good at shopping. And your name isn't Juan.

Man to whom I give my root, my belly, my mind,
my small joy divided among these ragged socks, unsewn
when you need to dress well . . .
What difference to you
that the children make their beds,
pick up their shoes
and help me dry the dishes
if you study for your next class
in the most comfortable chair we have
and keep your fear in shadow, almost hidden
so no one will discover that *macho* at the base of your spine!
And you make Revolution from the Five Year Plan
but as you can, straddling Rocinante
while Dulcinea admires your prowess, the lance, the windmills,
and you, in the neighborhood, defending the social advantages
of our new Constitution!
            You make Revolution:
      starched shirt,
      clean refrigerator,
      beds made,
      shining pots,
floors so clean you can eat or spit on them.

Well, no.

Go, search for yourself at the root. Grow.
No longer does everyone follow you.
The men of your time are of another breed,
      jump time and space.
Don't forget it when shame comes up
to plant the hypocrite kiss on your brow
and you run and hide the mop—company's come—
surprised at your own conditioning, comrade.

Now that your specialty
is breaking your balls for Future,
keep in mind
we're neither distance nor different lands,
winds of the same new world we are, reborn,
we're all October!
Learn then to heat your food while I study,
put your diplomas away,
all that coursework with honors,
take down the titles: doctor,
                        engineer,
                        journalist,
                        sailor
and—why not?—technician in loneliness,
                        architect of anguish.

Because Revolution is more than I want,
                        more than Party member,
                        more than Congress, Assembly
your eyelids closing over the book, the seed,
gun raised, fraternal death.

REVOLUTION

is also we who make and do
who plough with you,
who pencil, who trench . . .
Revolution is your hands once more
your warm voice when I'm tired,
you, seated next to my blood
as I wash the dishes
and the smile when duty calls
and we share the task of leaving our bed.

Revolution, my love, will also be
when day breaks one of these centuries
and pride strokes the militant home,
the honey in your hands turned sweet again.

Comrade, when the day breaks,
you'll have risen, finally,
TO THE HIGHEST HUMAN PLANE.

CHAPTER ONE

The Struggle Against Sexism

*"If men want us out working
they're going to have to get
to work in the home!"*
Woman factory worker during
an assembly in the plant,
Havana, 1973.

If you come to Cuba, you can meet women who played an important role in freeing their country from tyranny. You can speak with women who are twenty years into equal pay for equal work, full educational possibilities, and a control over their own bodies so ample it's never been an issue. You can share the experience of a sister who has cut 100,000 *arrobas*[1] of sugar cane, or who is Minister of Light Industry, or who is simply an ex-maid who joined the old Communist Party in 1943 "because the rich folks in our town said that was *bad*, and I figures if it was bad for them it was good for me!" You can talk to women who went to Angola as fighters or as teachers — or as both.

If you come to Cuba, you can also meet the woman who hasn't been able to shake the traditional idea that her "place" is in home and office both, and claims *pride* at carrying such a heavy load. If you come to Cuba and walk down the street, it probably won't be long before some guy whispers in your ear,

[1] An *arroba* is twenty-five pounds.

21

or shouts out a pat or ingenious epithet, which will be one more on his mental scoreboard for the day and one more frustration for you. All this might indeed confuse you. You might ask: Why do these contradictions persist, where is the consciousness about them, and what's being done about it all?

Women in the Insurrectional Period — Some History

Cubans and others writing about Cuba are fond of mentioning women such as Celia Sánchez (early rebel soldier adjacent to the Revolutionary General Staff, now member of the Central Committee of the Cuban Communist Party and Council of Ministers),[2] Vilma Espín (once head of the underground for the entire province of Oriente, now member of the Central Committee of the Party, member of the Council of State, and president of the Federation of Cuban Women), Haydée Santamaría and Melba Hernández (the two women involved in the 1953 attack on Moncada Barracks; now Santamaría is a member of the Central Committee of the Party, member of the Council of State, and director of the Casa de las Américas cultural institution,[3] while Hernández is Cuba's Ambassador to Vietnam). The Cuban war of liberation actually saw thousands of women anonymously involved in the revolutionary effort: selling war bonds and producing rebel uniforms, taking part in propaganda work, participating in action and sabotage units in the cities, transporting arms, and fighting in the mountains.

Toward the middle of the last year of the war, Fidel Castro encouraged the formation of the Mariana Grajales Platoon, made up of a dozen women whose tasks on the front lines had long been equivalent to fighting. The women got together and demanded their right to fight on equal terms with their brothers. The commander-in-chief of the rebel army was receptive to the idea, but there was resistance from his male officers. All the old ideas of "women fainting at the sight of blood," "women being too soft to really kill," and "women's maternal instincts," came

[2] Deceased, 1980.

[3] Committed suicide in 1980 shortly after a severe car occident which nearly took her life.

to the surface in these discussions, which were the first ideological discussions about women's full participation that we know about in the modern Cuban experience. Fidel was insistent, however, and he charged one of the most resistant, Major Eddy Suñol, with taking the newly formed women's platoon into battle. It was September 1958. By November, Suñol was proclaiming the bravery and precision of his new soldiers. The Marianas, as they were called, saw action in some twenty important battles before the enemy capitulated on New Year's Eve, and then they went on to enlarge their ranks and take on peacetime military tasks. In today's Cuban army there are thousands of women. Thelma Bornot, one of the original Marianas, has been elevated to the rank of major.

Urselia Díaz Baez, an eighteen year-old high school girl, died with a bomb in her hands in Havana's Cine América. Lydia Doce and Clodomira Ferrals Acosta were mountain messengers tortured to death by Batista's men on one of their missions to the capital city. The Giralt sisters, members of the underground, were gunned down coming home one night. Yet, when the war ended, Cuban men, and women too, reverted somewhat to the idea that "now that the time of sacrifice has ended, women may return to the home."

The Early Years

The revolution inherited a female labor force of around 194,000. Seventy percent of these women worked as domestic servants, with the accompanying long hours, oppressive conditions, lack of fringe benefits, and miserable pay. 700,000 men were unemployed and 300,000 underemployed, making plans for massively incorporating women into the labor force impossible. Women of differing backgrounds and ideologies, who shared their support for the revolution, their desire to help it consolidate and grow — as well as their need to make it work for them *as women* — came together in the Federation of Cuban Women (FMC) on August 23, 1960. This organization, enthusiastic and innovative from its beginnings, was responsible for silencing the bourgeois attempts at "empty pot" marches (the

Chileans weren't the first!). The Federation met with women from other Latin American countries to share experiences and ideas, and set about to take on the enormous tasks facing not only Cuban women, but the entire nation.

The FMC launched special schools for domestic servants and it was centrally involved in the plans for reeducation of prostitutes, schools for peasant women, and the dressmaking academies. Through these initiatives, women all over the island were encouraged to emerge from the very protective and limited home atmosphere to learn new skills as well as a new ideology.

Because of the high male unemployment rate, the FMC's first years were not dedicated to getting women into the labor market but to encouraging housewives to become involved in voluntary work where new disciplines and work habits might be developed. By 1964, with unemployment now a thing of the past, the priority was to incorporate women into the paid work force. In the next ten years, twenty-four percent of the productive and service forces became female and there was no longer a vast number of unfilled jobs. By then the needed workers were required to have much more advanced technological training. Not just any worker, but highly skilled workers were in demand. While continuing to encourage women to join the labor force, the FMC was also evolving specialized preparatory courses so that a greater number of women could compete for more technical and rewarding work.

Relatively soon after the triumph of 1959, Cuban universities were graduating women as more than half of their new doctors, over a third of their new engineers, and forty percent of their new architects. Thus, it was never a matter of women *not* entering the professions, but a much broader situation, involving hundreds of thousands of women whose history, for centuries, carried the load of illiteracy, unpaid drudgery, and dependency.

Of the quarter of Cuba's adult population which was illiterate when the rebels came to power, more than half were women, with the proportion rising steeply in the rural areas. Interestingly, in the giant literacy "army" of young people who swept across the island during 1961 and in one year eliminated this problem, fifty-six percent of the 100,000 volunteers were young girls. Consider for a moment what this meant in the lives of these young women: 56,000 girls between the ages of ten and eighteen went into the countryside, lived and shared the work in the difficult circumstances of 1961 rural Cuba; they faced the same risks as their brothers from CIA-backed counterrevolutionary bandits who took the literacy campaign as a signal to rape and murder, and they became highly proletarianized through their contact with Cuba's hardworking poor as they taught reading and writing. These were young girls who conventionally did not go out on a date without a chaperone! The intensely formative literacy brigade experience was to carry them a long way in their own liberation as well as that of their country.

Maids were becoming bank tellers in those days. Prostitutes were becoming translators and secretaries. Women who learned to write their own names at the age of thirty-five, with seven children, were becoming administrators of state farms, production chiefs in factories, and leadership cadres in mass and selective political organizations. Women headed schools, hospitals, cultural institutions, and began to stand out in sports and the arts. Women entered important decisionmaking positions on governing bodies and in the party. Yet women remained a minority in the ranks of the party and the Union of Young Communists, while women's participation in the labor force began to level off at the one-quarter mark.

Of course, this was partially a matter of economic logistics in a country whose priority was raising production levels in order to emerge more rapidly from underdevelopment. But, as is also true in these cases, economic logistics and real ideological contradictions, such as sexism, are rarely totally separate. There is an overlap, and this overlap itself tends to strengthen the sexual double standard unless there is a constant raising of consciousness about this problem.

Figures from 1979 show that thirty percent of the work force is now female and that trade union leadership, at the local level, is thirty-seven percent female. This is an interesting situation, as more women have prominent trade union roles than their labor force percentage would lead us to expect might be the case. The difference is probably due to added assertiveness on the part of those women. As we go up through the highest levels of national trade union leadership, the percentage of women in important positions diminishes, revealing that there are still problems with completely equal representation at the top. The Fourteenth Central Cuban Trade Workers Union (CTC) Congress was held in December 1978, resulting in the election of a new National Trade Union Council. Of its 144 members, twenty-six are women (eighteen percent). Three women are members of the Council's executive board, and one — Rosario Fernández — rose to the number three spot on that thirteen-member Secretariat. Four months after her election, Rosario Fernández summarized some of the achievements of the past twenty years and indicated some of the more immediate tasks:

> As far as women staying in the workforce, we've had our ups and down, but at the present moment we've reached a high level of stability (ninety-five percent). We've had to build up a whole material base for women to be able to get out to work, children's day-care centers, school lunch programs, workers' dining rooms, laundry and dry cleaning services, priority distribution of certain items to working women, etcetera, and we've also had to wage a battle against the vestiges of old male chauvinist attitudes. To the extent that we can broaden and develop the material base and wipe out old prejudices, we'll also see that thirty percent increase. Women joining the workforce have made a great contribution to the workers' movement, which has benefited in terms of cohesion, unity of action and maturity. And in the unions, women have gained a prestige which they well deserve.[4]

An even more interesting and optimistic situation can be seen if we examine the composition of the twenty new work commissions elected at the December 1978 session of the People's National Assembly. Each of these commissions has its president, vice-president, and secretary; and it is clear that these men and women will be playing vital roles in running the country. Statistically, five of the twenty presidents, four of the twenty vice-presidents, and eight of the twenty secretaries, are women, for a total of seventeen out of sixty (a little over twenty-eight percent). This is a good sign, as the percentage is already better than the twenty-five percent female representation in the Assembly as a whole. Even more interesting than the percentages

[4] "A Question for — Rosario Fernández," *Granma* (English edition), March 18, 1979, p. 7.

are the specific tasks to which the women involved have been assigned: Aleida March is president of the Foreign Relations Commission; Martha Lugioyo is the secretary of Constitutional and Judicial Affairs; Carmen de las N. Serrano is secretary of Health and Ecology; and Dalia Alelí García is secretary of Culture and Art; Education and Science has Nélida M. Novales as its vice-president and Edelmira Valle as its secretary; Reina E. Frómeta, Vera O. Bueno, and Luisa Casamichana are secretaries of Sports and Tourism, Labor and Social Security, and Foreign Commerce, Economic, Scientific and Technological Collaboration, respectively; Gudelia García is the vice-president of Domestic Commerce and Foodstuffs; Nieves Varona heads the commission of Industry, and Josefina J. Revellón heads Building and Building Materials, whose secretary is also a woman, Mireya E. Gaínza; the president and vice-president of the commission on Citizens' Complaints and Suggestions are Mercedes de la Cruz and Mercedes C. González; it is not unusual that the commission on Attention to Children and Women's Equality is headed by a woman, Vilma Espín, and that another woman, Marta Depréss, is vice-president of the same commission, but, inversely in this case, it might interest feminists from other countries to find out that Santiago Alvarez, the well-known filmmaker, is secretary of this commission set up to deal with, among other things, sexual inequality. Another example of women's increasing role in national level leadership can be seen in the outcome of the elections for the national secretariat of the Federation of University Students in March 1979. Of the nine-member secretariat, four are now women.

By going back but a few years, we can see that attitudes are changing fast. When I did the interviews for *Cuban Women Now*, in 1970 and 1971, many women told me they saw their role as a dual one: they were proud to be exceling at work and in a variety of political and mass organizations while carrying the complete household and child care role. Some said their husbands helped, but few expressed the conviction that help would have to become a real sharing process. Women doing extraordinary tasks in the fields, women whose cane-cutting abilities warranted flowing press coverage, showed me carefully manicured fingernails beneath their cutter's gloves. Only one woman, working in a foundry in Matanzas, expressed the idea that, "These hands of mine are beautiful in a new kind of way, a proletarian beauty. . . ." On the streets, women generally accepted, albeit pretended not to hear, the grunts and commentary; and, in fact, they saw diminishing return of that kind of attention as a sign that "they were not looking their best today" or that they were "getting old." Today's attitudes, at least expressed if not yet always reflected in total life styles, are very different.

In March of 1968, Articles 47 and 48 of the Cuban Labor Code were passed, stipulating some 500 posts closed to women for reasons of health connected with the female reproductive system. Another 500 were reserved for women only. These were attempts to rationalize the labor force in an economy desperately trying to counteract the effects of the blockade imposed by the United States, while dragging itself up from centuries of underdevelopment. FMC cadres went out and discussed the country's production needs with thousands of men, convincing many who were working in light industry or other physically less strenuous tasks to relinquish their positions to women and themselves take on heavier physical labor. 25,000 men switched jobs as a result of this campaign. At the same time, these cadres visited over 400,000 women in their homes, persuading many of them to enter sectors of industry and services in jobs considered physically compatible with their sex. It should be noted that neither administrative nor pay differentials resulted from this compartmentalization. The ideological consequences were complex, to say the least.

In the 1970 interviews, I asked these questions over and over again: "What do you think of Articles 47 and 48?" "Do you think a woman can do the same work as a man, physically speaking?" Similar answers, in general, came from professional women, peasants, and workers. Many had never heard of Articles 47 and 48. Cane-cutters laughed when told their specialty was on the prohibited list! This and many similar situations seemed to uphold the assertion that these clauses in the labor code were written to protect women from having to go into occupations they would find exploitative as well as to rationalize the distribution of workers. Women who wanted to cut cane and load heavy sacks, and who were found to be productive at that type of work, were never actually *prevented* from doing so. Many peasant women just thought my question curious or irrelevant. They and their ancestors had been doing such things all their lives. They saw it as normal work for which they might now, happily, be paid. Nevertheless, the consensus still seemed to be that, in Cuba, differences between men's and women's roles were thought to be biological as well as social in origin. In 1974, Articles 47 and 48 were repealed, but in 1976 more moderate, although similar, controls were put into effect.

For a woman to work and enjoy the same possibilities for advancement available to her brothers in a society where it will be a long time before men really take on half the household load, ample facilities must be provided by the state in order at least to eliminate the rough edges of domestic inequality. In fact, the socialist goal is *not* that individual men or women continue to do these tasks, but that they become collectivized, socialized.

Before 1959, there were virtually no day care centers in Cuba, only a few *creches*[5] run by charity organizations, which were patronized and used by the upper classes. The FMC saw day care as one of its immediate and most important tasks. From among the domestic servants learning skills for more dignified jobs, 1,000 were selected to train as the first day care workers. Mansions left by the fleeing bourgeoisie were adapted as *circulos*.[6] Four-month crash courses in the early years when the priority had to be simply to staff the schools gradually gave way, in 1969, to day care teacher-training institutes. In Havana, Las Villas, and Santiago, three geographically strategic spots across the island, personnel take a four-year course that includes psychology, dietetics, corporal movement, pedagogy, and other specializations. Cuban day care centers receive infants from as young as forty-five days, to correspond with the termination of paid maternity leave three months after delivery, to six years old. In 1965, the nominal fee was eliminated, making day care free, as is all education in Cuba. In 1977, a nominal fee, on a sliding scale according to family income, was reinstated. The child is fed, clothed, and receives complete medical attention, including dental

[5] Infant care facilities.
[6] Developmentally-oriented child care centers.

treatment, and, if necessary, psychiatric services, as well as the initial stages of a scientific education.

At this writing, there are close to 800 day care centers across the island, serving areas with the greatest numbers of working mothers. More than 86,000 children are cared for and educated in these institutions. Although a priority of the revolution, as can be seen by the number of new *círculos* constantly being built and staffed, it must be understood that the economy has not yet been able to support enough of these centers to provide day care to all pre-school children. Preference at this point is naturally given to children whose mothers work. This is both a stimulus for women to enter the salaried labor force and a barrier to all those not working who might otherwise be able to. In many cases, grandmothers or elderly aunts, and occasionally grandfathers or elderly uncles, provide this important service in what can only be considered a temporary and transitional solution.

For Cubans, the primary goal of day care is to educate children. Secondarily, the centers are established to free mothers to work. When there are finally enough centers to accommodate all Cuban youngsters, the current preference given working mothers will no longer be necessary. The first Five Year Plan calls for the construction of 400 more *círculos*.

Other social services have been developed over these twenty years of change: almost all work places either have their own dining room or share a workers' dining room at a nearby center. Grade school children from homes where both adults work have access to hot lunch programs at school. All primary schools have a mid-morning and a mid-afternoon snack for the entire student body. Beginning at the junior high school level, there is an increasing amount of optional education in the boarding school system, where students live at school all week and come home on weekends. Women workers often have laundry services connected with their work places and new automatic laundromats have opened in residential neighborhoods. A special shopping-bag plan (Plan Jaba), in effect for close to ten years, has greatly reduced time-consuming lines for families where all adults work. All these plans, however, are still in the process of being implemented to their full and necessary capacity.

A Turning Point

The foregoing has been a very schematic summary of women's pre-revolutionary, insurrectional, and early revolutionary situations in Cuba. It sets a basic context for a more detailed examination of what happened in 1974, its consequences, and implications.

After the 1959 victory, the soldiers who had fought a successful war of liberation were faced with the myriad problems of running a country. Government offices often started practically from scratch after junking the rampant corruption and class privileges of the old regime. Gradually, the new Communist Party, organized in 1965 from the ranks of the old Partido Socialista Popular, the Student Directorate, and Fidel's 26th of July Movement, took on an overload of responsibility in government. Several faulty experiments in the organization of the economy and some false starts and reevaluations were climaxed by failure to reach the goal of ten million tons of sugar in the 1970 harvest. This setback was turned to an advantage. "Turn the setback to victory" was, in fact, the motto of the courageous and determined Cuban people following that experience. The government began a greater democratization of the trade union movement, with increased participation by workers in decisions concerning production. This reorganization was completed toward the end of 1973. Marxist philosophy and economics were offered in systematized courses to large sectors of the population, not only to those studying at specific academic levels. Mass participation in voluntary organizations such as the Revolutionary Defense Committees (CDR), with over three million members, and the FMC, with close to two million women, continued. People took part in active discussions of all the important drafts of new laws through these organizations and in schools, military units, and trade unions.

The great evolution was the development of a highly democratic system of people's government, *Poder Popular*, or people's power. Local delegates were elected by the people at the grass roots level. A Municipal Assembly would then elect both the Provincial and the National Assemblies from among its own ranks, and the National Assembly would then begin to function as the supreme governing body of the land. Neighborhood nominations were handled in open meetings, where prolonged discussion of each candidate was thorough and followed by direct show-of-hands voting. A single eight-by-ten inch photograph and a one-page typed personal history of each of these elected candidates then was placed in a designated window where all could see, remaining there until election day. On election day, the secret ballot urns were guarded by the Pioneers,[7] schoolchildren who are between six to fourteen! This system, now in its second year nation-wide, is revolutionizing an already popular government. It seeks to lay the foundations for a communist future in a transitional socialist present.

The process I have just described was tried out first in one of the original six provinces,[8] Matanzas. If was felt that a one-year pilot plan and the experience gained from it would aid a smooth transition nationally. Every July 26, Fidel speaks in a different part of the country. The 1974 commemoration was held in Matanzas, precisely because of the People's Power experiment, and the new governance process formed the bulk of Fidel's speech. The country's honored guest at those July 26 festivities was Nguyen Thi Dinh, perhaps the only woman in the world at that moment in the leadership of an important liberation army[9] Nguyen Thi Dinh was a Vietnamese peasant woman who had learned to read and write as a young adult! Fidel, after pointing to the extraordinarily low percentage of women delegates (3%) and using the election to back up his assertion that women still suffered discrimination in Cuba, singled out Madam Dinh and said:

[7] The Pioneer Movement is a voluntary mass organization for children. Almost all young people in Cuba belong, and, through it, are involved in cultural, athletic, patriotic, political, and recreational activities. Members are gradually assigned small tasks. By the time a child is fourteen, conduct, attitude, and a sense of responsibility in handling these assignments, provide a tangible evaluatory base as to who is chosen for membership in the Young Communist Movement.

[8] Cuba was divided into six provinces until the political, economic, and administrative reorganization of the country which was put into effect concurrent with the establishment of People's Power. The new organization divides the country into fourteen provinces with 169 municipalities. Bureaucracy was reduced by eliminating the regional division.

[9] Nglyen Thi Dinh was Vice-Commander-in-Chief of the South Vietnamese Liberation Army.

An example of the importance of women in the struggle for liberation and the importance of women's qualities—we have such an example right here in comrade Nguyen Thi Dinh, Vice-Commander of the People's Liberation Army of South Vietnam. There she is! . . .

And we have abundant examples of women like this in the history of our own country, of our own revolution, the attack on Moncada Barracks and in our own war in the Sierra Maestra. Enough said in terms of the self-criticism we can make. Of course, we're not going to be able to resolve this situation overnight, but we must be conscious of the need to struggle against these remnants of the past, and all the people must participate in the struggle: men and women together. And women in the forefront!

It is important to note that this is not a concern that began and ended with Fidel. Here, as in so many other cases, his words were simply a reflection and projection of a concern manifested principally by women throughout the ranks of the Federation. Fidel went on to suggest that a multidisciplinary study be made of the results of the Matanzas elections to find out why such a small number of women had been elected.

The results of this study were that women, in one way or another, already expected to work a double shift, were not anxious to be loaded down with any further obligations! A real nation-wide consciousness around this old problem emerged as a result of Fidel's speech and the follow-up study. Throughout 1975, when the Cuban people got together to discuss the number of theses to be presented at the First Communist Party Congress in December, one of the most important was "Thesis Number Three: On Exercising Women's Full Equality," to which the result of the aforementioned study was appended.

"Thesis Three," as it was called, became study material in work places, schools from the junior high school level and up, military units, peasant bases, CDRs, and Federation grass roots units.[10] In many mixed centers, women were encouraged to study the material separately first, in order to assure full participation and suggestions. In these cases, study by men and women followed the first all-female discussion. "Thesis Three" was only one link in a many-sided campaign launched to deal with what Fidel began

[10] See Appendix I for the English translation of "Thesis Three."

to call the subjective remnants of discrimination. At the same time, the country was discussing, amending, and finally voting on the new Family Code. The FMC's Second Congress was held in November 1974, and this, too, naturally became a context for profound study of all these questions by close to 2,000 delegates from all over the country. Battling sexism began to acquire policy status.

A Three-Pronged Campaign: FMC Congress, Family Code, and Thesis Three

Only four months had passed from the time of Fidel's twenty-sixth of July speech when the Federation of Cuban Women held its Second Congress in November 1974. The depth of the discussions and the profundity of the papers presented by different delegations to that Congress indicate that the new consciousness was not simply derived from Fidel's specific warning but was an ongoing grass roots level concern of the women themselves.

I'll never forget the atmosphere at that Congress, which I was privileged to attend as a journalist. It was the most intense combination of seriousness, audacity, and exaltation I've witnessed among women here. In a matter of minutes, in the theater of the Central Cuban Trade Workers Union, one might see an all-female conga line swinging and singing its joy; or hear a complex and demanding intervention from a delegate who may have gone hours on horseback to get to the bus stop for transportation to the special train that brought women from the length and breadth of the country; or partake of the deafening cheers greeting Angela Davis, Valentina Tereshkova,[11] and women from Laos, Vietnam, and Africa.

Fidel opened the Congress, and he stayed all day long for all five days. It was clear that he understood his role was to listen and to learn. He took notes — in preparation, no doubt — for his closing speech on November 29, which might explain its special relevance.

[11] Soviet cosmonaut.

The women discussed the need for deeper and more socially-linked sex education in the schools, beginning at the earliest grades. They demanded analysis of the image of women projected in the mass media and laid the groundwork for many changes in that area. The problem of the second shift was amply aired. Vilma Espín, president of the Federation, read a lengthy and detailed report on FMC work — problems as well as achievements — since its foundation on August 23, 1960. One of the most noteworthy aspects of the event was the consistency with which delegates and others were encouraged to speak their minds completely. In order that one delegate might have a satisfactory answer to her question about a problem with the schools, Fidel called the Minister of Education, who made an immediate appearance to deal with a series of complaints.

It might be interesting here to briefly note something about the 1,916 women representing their 1,932,422 sisters nation-wide. In terms of age, eleven percent were between fourteen and twenty-five, forty-five percent were between twenty-six and forty, and forty-four percent were over forty years of age. Seventy-eight percent were working women, one percent students, two percent retired, and nineteen percent housewives. Forty-seven percent were members of the Cuban Communist Party, nine percent held membership in the Young Communist Union, one hundred percent belonged to the FMC, ninety-seven percent to the Revolutionary Defense Committees, three percent to the ANAP (National Association of Small Farmers), fifty-nine percent were trade union members, and eighty-six percent belonged to the Revolutionary Militia. As for educational levels, fifty percent had finished primary school, thirty percent were graduates of junior high school, fourteen percent had completed high school, five percent had university degress, and one percent had postgraduate diplomas. Forty percent of the delegates came from the leadership levels within the women's organization, and the other sixty percent from the grass roots level.

Theses on the housewife, the woman worker, the young woman, the peasant woman, the role of the family in socialist society, solidarity with women and their struggles around the world, and the organization's new statutes and by-laws were debated by commissions. These commissions met during the Congress, and the theses as well as the resolutions were read and approved by the floor in plenary meetings. It is important to note the FMC's shift in emphasis at this time (1974) from merely getting women into the salaried labor force to increasing women's participation in specialized training courses, thereby qualifying them to hold more decisionmaking and leadership posts. One of the primary concerns in this Congress was articulated in the following portion of Fidel's extremely important closing speech:

> ... Of course women in the socialist countries have gone a long way toward their liberation. But if we question our own particular situation: we, a socialist country, with almost sixteen years of revolution behind us, can we really claim that Cuban women, in practice, have achieved full and equal rights and that they are totally integrated into Cuban society?
>
> We might analyze, for example, a few figures. Before the revolution there were 194,000 women working. Of these, as was pointed out in one of the reports here, seventy percent were domestic servants. Today, we have three times that many women working. The figure for women working in the civilian sector—which, as you know, includes the majority of production, service, and administrative workers—is 590,000 out of a total of 2,331,000 persons employed. That is to say, over twenty-five percent of our workers are women. Nevertheless, the number of women who hold leadership positions throughout this whole apparatus of production, services, and administration, is only fifteen percent. In our party, female militancy is barely thirteen percent, a notably low figure. And only six percent of the party's full-time professional cadres are women.
>
> But we have an even more explicit example, related to the elections of People's Power delegates in the province of Matanzas. The number of women nominated comprised 7.6 percent, and those elected only three percent. The comrade from Matanzas spoke about this.
>
> These figures should really concern us, move us to raise our consciousness around this problem. Because in these elections the candidates were nominated by the masses and the masses only proposed 7.6 percent women candidates when women make up approximately fifty percent of the population. And the masses elected only three percent women delegates.
>
> Who among those who have witnessed this Congress, who

among the invited guests who have shared this week with us, could suppose or imagine or conceive of the fact that with such a strong and politically advanced women's movement, in elections such as those mentioned, only three percent women could be elected?

And what does this data reflect? The fact that, after more than fifteen years of revolution, in this respect we are still politically and culturally backward. The fact is that there are still objective and subjective factors maintaining a discriminatory situation regarding women. . . .

The objective factors to the economic base — day care facilities and other social services — and to the judicial system are rapidly being renovated and reformed. The subjective factors can be summed up by the word coined by sisters in the developed countries, sexism. A new consciousness was developing around the old Latin *machismo.*

The Family Code

The Family Code began to be discussed by the Cuban people early in 1974, and the original idea was that it become law in time for the FMC Congress. At the same time, the importance of this code made it imperative that discussions be thorough and far-reaching. Blas Roca, now a member of the party's Politburo and president of the National People's Assembly and then member of the party's Secretariat and head of the committee to draft new laws, spoke at the Women's Congress and explained the process of debate and discussion. He noted tendencies, offered anecdotes about ingrained unconscious sexism on the part of leadership, and made a plea for long-term ideological work in this respect. He told us how junior high school students were discussing the law, the first law to be discussed by this age group because of its importance to their future. He brought statistics from the discussions held by Cuban diplomatic delegations overseas, military units, and comrades involved in international missions.

The Code, like all of Cuba's most important laws, had been published in draft form in a cheap tabloid edition so that

virtually every man, woman, and young person could have a copy
to read and study. In meetings through the trade unions, the
CDRs, the FMC, the schools, and the like, people have a chance—
often more than one chance, as most citizens attend more than
one of these meetings — to discuss the Code point by point, ask
questions, suggest additions, changes, or deletions. The way this
process works is that a record is kept of each meeting, the results
are sent through the respective organizations to their highest
level, where they are tabulated, computed, and turned over to
the original committee (adjacent, at that time, to the party's
Central Committee, now adjacent to the National Assembly).
The Code is then modified according to the people's attitudes
around specific issues and their participation in this process. For
example, in the original draft of the Family Code, the marriage
age for men had been higher than that for women. The people
made them the same. The Code was finally returned to the Cuban
people on International Women's Day, March 8, 1975.

The Family Code covers marriage, divorce, marital property
relationships, recognition of children, obligations for children's
care and education, adoption, and tutelage. Basically, the Code
stipulates a new equality between women and men in their social
relationships. Child support is not now automatically expected
of the man, but, instead, might be expected of the woman in
cases where the man is studying and the woman working. Custody
of children is not given over to one parent or another, but provisions are sought through which both must continue to assume
responsibilities in the event of divorce.

The clauses in this Code receiving the most attention and
discussion are those stipulating both parents' equal responsibilities for child care and housework. The five clauses (24 through
28) covering this aspect have also been incorporated into the
Cuban marriage ceremony and are read by judges performing all
civil marriages, the only kind recognized by Cuban law.

Clauses 24, 25, 26, 27, and 28 read as follows:

24) Marriage is constituted on the basis of equal rights and
duties of both spouses.

25) The spouses must live together, be faithful to one another,
consider and respect each other and each mutually help
the other.

The rights and duties established by this Code will subsist in their entirety as long as the marriage has not been legally terminated, in spite of the fact that for justifiable reasons a common household cannot be maintained.

26) Both spouses are obligated to care for the family they have created and cooperate with each other in the education, formation and guidance of their children in line with the principles of socialist morality. As well, each to the extent of his or her capabilities and possibilities, must participate in governing the home and cooperate toward its best possible care.

27) The spouses are obliged to contribute toward satisfying the needs of the family they have created in their marriage, each according to his or her faculties and economic capacities. Nevertheless, if one of the spouses contributes only through his or her work in the home and child-care, the other spouse must provide full economic support without this meaning that he or she be relieved of the obligations of cooperating with the housework and child-care.

28) Both spouses have the right to exercise their professions or crafts and must lend each other reciprocal cooperation and aid to this effect, as well as in order to carry out studies or perfect their training, but in all cases they will take care to organize their home life so that such activities be coordinated with the fulfillment of the obligations imposed by this Code.

How does this Code work in practice? That's the question asked by most visitors to Cuba, and many seem to imply that, unless an overnight close-to-total change be effected, the Code doesn't work.

The Family Code is a law. It is also an educational tool. At this point, I believe the latter is the most important of the two aspects. The very discussions over the period of eight months when people grappled with these ideas stimulated an emerging consciousness or gave voice to a series of previously unarticulated concepts. The discussions were not only those officially staged by the political and mass organizations; some of the most intense took place on buses, in waiting rooms, in supermarket lines, and on the streets!

One example of this occurred in the discussion held through the CDR on my block. An elderly male neighbor had this to say:

"You know ... I've always believed in helping my wife. We've been married a long time, and I cook, clean, have taken care of our children and our grandchildren ... but one thing I never felt right about doing was hanging the clothes on the line. I was afraid people would see me and laugh. Now I guess the time has come to get over these complexes.... We're all in this together!" In a second incident, in our local supermarket, one day when Family Code discussions were at their height, a man in the meat line mumbled something about "... this really is women's work.... Women are so good at this kind of thing...!" A woman directly in front of him turned around, and, with her face as close to his as possible, responded: "... and some men are good at eating shit!"

The judicial repercussions of the Code, needless to say, depend on women themselves actually taking their husbands to court for violations. How many women are willing to take this step? Not enough. Clearly, many, for a long time to come, will allow themselves to be conned by the dozens of mechanisms men all over the world have developed to keep things the way they have always been. The important thing, at this point, is that women have state and party support in their struggle. A woman can go to the president of her CDR, or to the leadership of her own or her husband's trade union, and she has a legal, and not simply a subjective, basis on which to request help in an unequal home situation. There are no statistics familiar to me of cases actually brought before judges. In close observation of this whole process, I think it is fair to say that in places like the Isle of Youth, where many young couples live and work without the proverbial grandmother or aunt in the house, there is a stronger definition and a more aggressive attitude on the part of the women than, say, in situations where it is easier to fall back on the oppression of older retired, mostly female, family members.

It's also important to note that prevalent attitudes around these issues vary greatly from the older to the younger generations. Cuban young people, provided with a new and more progressive type of education than their parents and grandparents, view sexual equality as a normal, natural part of their lives. Speaking with junior and senior high school students, you won't find many young women who see their futures dependent on marriage or a future husband's career. Their central goal in life is their own development and their potential contribution to society.

My own two teenage daughters and their friends expect absolute agreement and support from boy friends around their logical political participation, and they insist upon full social integration at all levels. One of my daughters attends a special school, the Lenin School, for above-average students going into scientific and technological fields. Of the 4,500 students, slightly more than half are young women. Girls excel in the traditionally male areas such as math, physics, chemistry, and biology. Several years ago at this school, some of the boys in one of the dorms tried to get their girl friends to wash and iron their uniforms. This was clearly a ploy for status control. It wasn't only the small group of girls approached who resisted and refused, but, within days, a movement had developed through which the vast majority of the school's female students made it clear that this was an issue of principle for them all — a case of spontaneous ideology in action!

Although the law states that Family Code articles 24 through 28 are applicable only in cases where a man's wife works or studies, Vilma Espín, at a press conference following the official establishment of this Code, took the issue quite a bit further. She emphasized the fact that, although legally the Code only applies in the aforementioned cases, it will be important for *all* men, whether or not their wives remain in or work outside the home, to share these obligations. This will be the only way, she pointed out, that future generations will grow up with a new morality gleaned from a changed image of how men and women should interact.

Thesis Three is not a law, but a thesis from the First Party Congress. It was discussed by men and women and young people throughout the country, irrespective of their membership in the Party, and it reflects the thoughts of society's ideological vanguard around the issue of women's equality. Thesis Three goes much further than the Family Code, dealing with more difficult and complex issues. Some of these concerns are conjugal fidelity versus party membership, women traditionally being expected to follow their husbands when they are transfered from one city to another without regard for the women's own work, and the problem of young women becoming pregnant and dropping out of school.

Party members (two percent of the Cuban population — some 250,000 men and women out of a population of nine and a half million) are expected to be exemplary in every way, to be looked up to by their sisters and brothers, and to be people one may feel one can go to with problems. Since infidelity is considered negative in Cuban society, party members whose wives or husbands were known to be having affairs with men or women outside their marital relationship have always been requested to put an end to this kind of a situation. In short, they were asked to dissolve the secondary relationship, dissolve the marriage, or, if either of these solutions was impossible, leave the party. *In practice,* this kind of pressure was consistently applied to women, but almost never to men. The issue was in the air, and people expected it to be dealt with in some way in Thesis Three. But many were not prepared for the sophistication and profundity with which it was approached. Rather than taking the expected view that the traditional criteria be applied to men and women without distinction as to sex, the Thesis suggested that a person's sex life is a personal matter which should not affect party status! The resolution passed during the Congress stipulates:

> . . . Exploitation, parasitism, individualism, dishonesty, injustice, discrimination and inequality are immoral. The principles of socialist morality are identical for all citizens and it is therefore unjust that different criteria be applied when so-called "moral problems" are discussed regarding sexual relations. Men and women must be equally responsible in determining their relationships in the area of sexual life. Relationships in socialism must be based on equality, sincerity, and mutual respect.

In another part of the resolution, the inherited tendency to objectify women is attacked. Cuba has long been a nation without commercial advertising, where one would be hard put to find a feminine smile selling toothpaste or a female body selling a car. On the other hand, this kind of objectification has not been entirely erased from mass media. The resolution says:

> The First Party Congress considers it necessary to eliminate the

tendency of making women an object of exhibition, as is usual in the capitalist societies, and demands making all necessary efforts in order to guarantee that all night club acts and shows of a recreational nature, without implying loss of their characteristic tone, maintain an artistic quality and content in line with our current concepts in this respect. We recommend that the aforementioned tendency be eliminated from these shows, above all in the carnivals, in consideration of the fact that it is an activity all our people participate in.

As this thesis and resolution reflect the most advanced Cuban thought on these questions, I think it important to quote from the first paragraphs of the resolution, where the party ideology is most clearly stated:

The revolution, having achieved the country's real independence and sovereignty, abolished private property over the fundamental means of production and, setting out to construct socialism, created the basis for the realization of equality among all citizens. Consequently, equality of rights between men and women has risen since the revolutionary victory of January 1st, has been consecrated in our laws and in the Socialist Constitution our people approved in referendum as well as in our Party's Programmatic Platform as one of our Organization's invariable principles.

Nevertheless, situations of inequality persist, not only due to material difficulties which will be eradicated in the process of our economic development, but because quite frequently criteria and attitudes are maintained which are not in line with the principles and laws of our socialist society. . . .

The struggle for the full implementation of the equality of women is a task for our whole society, it is on the economic and cultural agendas, it requires the efforts of the Party and of the state, of administration and schools, of the Union of Young Communists and the social and mass organizations, among these and very specifically of the Federation of Cuban Women and the Cuban Workers Center, because as Fidel pointed out in the Second Congress of the FMC:

"This struggle against the discrimination of women, this struggle for women's equality and for women's integration is something the whole society must carry forward. And it is a task in the first place for our Party, it is a task for our educational institutions and it is a task for our mass organizations. In order to achieve these goals men and women must struggle together, men and women together must come to a profound and serious consciousness of this problem.

"Together we must wage this battle. And we are sure that it will be waged and that it will be won."

At this First Party Congress, a draft of Cuba's first socialist constitution was approved. This draft was then submitted to the people for discussion in the same kind of, by now traditional, process through which all important laws are made. As a result of this broad popular debate, the preamble and sixty of the 141 articles were modified in one way or another. On February 15, 1976, a special national referendum was held and 95.7% percent of all citizens, sixteen years or older (5,602,973 persons), declared their approval by way of secret ballot.

Articles dealing with women's place in society run throughout this new constitution. They are further evidence of the ongoing concern and struggle around basic rights concerning both sexes.

Article 8: The Socialist State:

b) as People's Power and serving the people themselves, guarantees that no man or woman, capable or working, be denied a place in the labor force through which he or she may contribute to society and to his or her own needs. . . .

Article 35: Marriage is a voluntary union between a man and a woman who are legally capable of taking this step, in order to live together. Marriage rests on absolutely equal rights and obligations of both spouses, both of whom must attend to the home and the integral formation of all children through their common effort, in a way in which this be compatible with the social activities of both.

Article 36: All children enjoy equal rights, whether they be conceived inside or outside marriage. All labels indicating illegitimacy are abolished.

Article 40: All citizens enjoy equal rights and are subject to equal duties.

Article 41: Discrimination for reasons of race, color, sex or national origin is prohibited and punishable by law.

Article 43: Women enjoy the same economic, political, social and family rights as men. In order to guarantee these rights and especially women's incorporation into the labor force, the state will see to it that women receive positions compatible with their physical constitution; paid maternity leave will be granted them before and after delivery; the state will organize institutions such as day care, semiboarding schools and boarding schools and will make all other efforts directed toward creating all the conditions which propitiate this principle of equality.

Article 135: All Cubans, men and women sixteen years of age and above, are eligible to vote.

Article 136: Cuban citizens, men or women, with full political rights, are eligible to be elected to office.

Conclusions

Socialism is not in itself an automatic end to sexual discrimination, but it is a necessary prerequisite to winning the battle against all forms of inequality. While economic equality is achieved through the abolition of antagonistic social classes, the class struggle persists in the superstructure: ideas and attitudes must be dealt with. This is the ongoing ideological struggle of which the struggle against sexism must be an important part. This is a task which men and women must engage in together under the leadership of politically aware women. In Cuba, after twenty years of socialist revolution, women have come a long way from their pre-revolutionary position of lack of education, nominal work possibilities, objectivization, subservience, and other forms of exploitation and oppression.

The nation's highest governing body, the National People's Assembly, less than three years from the initial attack on the low level of female participation in the Matanzas Assembly, can now claim twenty-five percent women delegates, a figure proportional to the thirty percent of women in the salaried labor force. Women's representation on the Central Committee of the party, on the State Council, and on the Council of Ministers has increased slightly. The percentages are not yet what they must be, but the direction is clear and determined.

The second national election for municipal People's Power delegates was held in April 1979. While nearly ninety-seven percent of eligible voters went to the polls, the results were disappointing in that, despite a great number of women candidates nominated, there was not a real increase in women delegates elected. A breakdown of provincial returns is revealing: in the province of the city of Havana, where the cultural level is still undeniably higher, over eighteen percent of the delegates were women, as opposed to four to five percent for some of the least populated and most heavily peasant areas. The outcome is certainly due to a complex variety of causes, not just to a generally lower cultural and educational level. There is also a great difference in life styles. People in the rural regions frequently live quite far from one another, and the women work very hard outside the salaried labor force as volunteers. In the new peasant communities, life is changing at an unbelievably fast rate, and women's votes are shifting just as quickly. For example, these women often constitute a higher proportion of paid workers than the national average.

The following incident occurred on my block during the nominating process for candidates to People's Power in 1976. The grass roots voting area, in this case, was made up of three different CDRs or block committees. Members of our CDR, several weeks before the important meeting, began to express our desire that our own CDR president, a very exceptional leader, an older black man who had been outstanding in the neighborhood for years, win the nomination. So certain were many of us of his merits that we began kidding him, calling him "delegate," and he joined in the kidding, naturally happy and proud.

When the evening of the district meeting arrived, we met with the members of the other two CDRs, and a number of nominations were made besides our own. People got up to talk about their nominees. Gradually, we began to notice that one woman was receiving exceptional attention. The two most frequently repeated adjectives used to describe her were "efficient" and "modest." Trutié Tisbé Matilla, who was a forty-four year-old woman with an eighth grade education, had been a founder of the 26th of July Movement in Guantanamo, fought on Raúl Castro's Second Front, ran a campaign hospital in the mountains during the war, and was now the administrator of a nursing school here in Havana and a member of the party, was clearly a nominee to be reckoned with.

After a half hour or so of discussion, our CDR president requested the floor and got up to speak. He talked about how much he had wanted to be nominated as a delegate, not for personal reasons but in order to better serve his neighbors. He talked about the joking, the label, the atmosphere on the block over the past several weeks. But he also went back to a speech of Fidel's in which the Cuban commander-in-chief had said that when a job arises, and a man and a woman have equal qualifications for that job, it should always be given to the woman just to try to even things up a bit. The president of our CDR went on to say that, in this case, he didn't believe it was even a question of equal qualifications; he felt Trutié was more qualified than he was and for that reason wanted to withdraw his name from the nominee list.

The people wouldn't let him withdraw his name. The CDR had nominated him and members felt he should be included in the vote. Not a few of us felt tears come to our eyes before the man stopped talking. Trutié won by a large majority. She later won elections at the municipal level and again at the provincial level to the National Assembly, where she is also one of the more than 100 women on that governing body. Here, in our district, her leadership has been excellent.

FMC poster, International Women's Day 1979: "Woman: Firm, Forever Fighting and Revolutionary."

Left: FMC poster, International Women's Day 1966.
Right: FMC poster, 1975: "Study and You Will Be an Active Part of the Future.'

FMC poster, 1969: "Your Work is Necessary."

POR UN 8 DE MARZO
DE SOLIDARIDAD MILITANTE
CON TODAS LAS MUJERES
DEL MUNDO

8 de Marzo
Día Internacional
de la Mujer

XV ANIVERSARIO DE LA F.M.C.
AGOSTO 23-1975

HACIA EL PRIMER CONGRESO
LUCHANDO POR LA IGUALDAD
PLENA DE LA MUJER

Left: FMC poster, International Women's Day, no date: "For a March 8th of Militant Solidarity with Women Around the World."
Right: FMC poster, 1975: "Toward the First Congress Struggling for Women's Full Equality."

Top: People's Power nominees. Havana.
Bottom: Sisters and CDR wall mural in Juanelo, Havana.

Top: Antonia Eiriz (standing right) teaching *papier mâche* to CDR members in Juanelo, Havana.
Bottom: CDR member on civilian guard duty in Cerro, Havana.

Top: Microbrigade worker setting tile in elementary school building. Alamar.
Bottom: Dr. Dolores Ochoa, Administrator-Pharmacist. Havana.

Top: Worker drying tobacco, near Güira de Melena.
Bottom: Workers assembling dry-cell batteries in factory housed in the Lenin School, near Havana.

Thelvia Marin, sculptor. Havana.

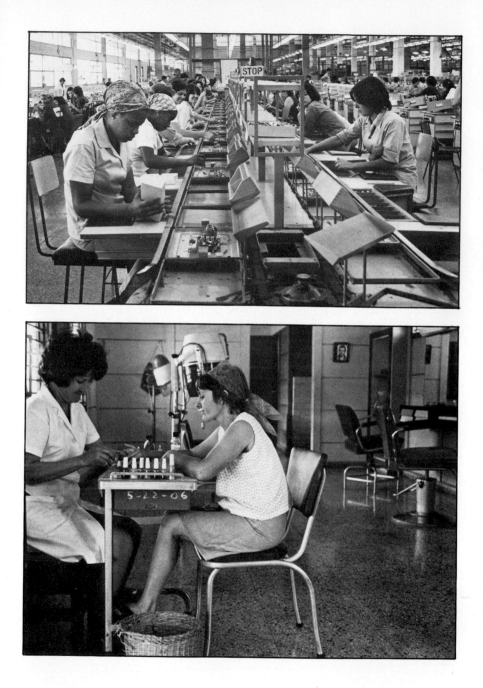

Top: Work-study students at the Lenin School electronics factory, near Havana.
Bottom: Manicure. Bentre Village.

Top: Public health volunteer preparing innoculations. San Antonio de los Baños.
Bottom: Microbrigade worker operating construction lift at elementary school building. Alamar.

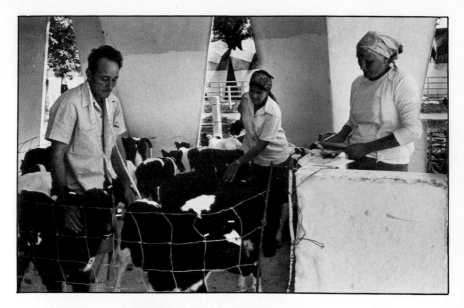

Top: Dairy workers at Bentre Village.
Bottom: Microbrigade worker polishing floors in elementary school building.
Alamar.

Havana Symphony Orchestra cellist rehearsing. Havana.

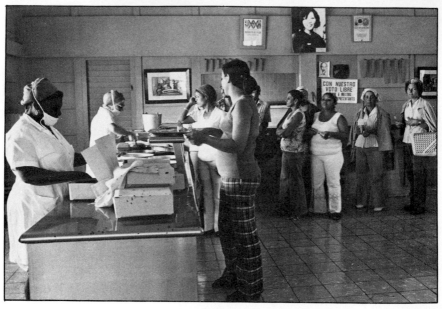

Top: Pharmacy technician. Havana.
Bottom: Workers' cafeteria. Bentre Village.

Top: Exercise class at the José Martí gymnasium. Havana.
Bottom: (Left to right) Hedy Villegas, actress; daughter Vilma Valles; and mother Iresema Mesa, singer, at Coppelia ice cream parlor. Havana.

Top: Former colonial palace in Prado now used for civil marriage ceremonies. Havana.
Bottom: Traditional approach to housework in Vedado, Havana.

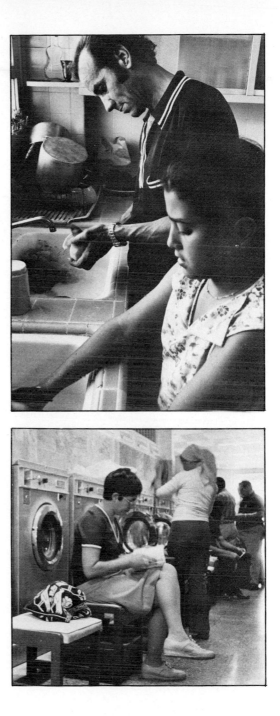

Top: Contemporary approach to dinner preparation in Vedado, Havana.
Bottom: New neighborhood laundromat in Vedado, Havana.

Couple at home in Vedado, Havana.

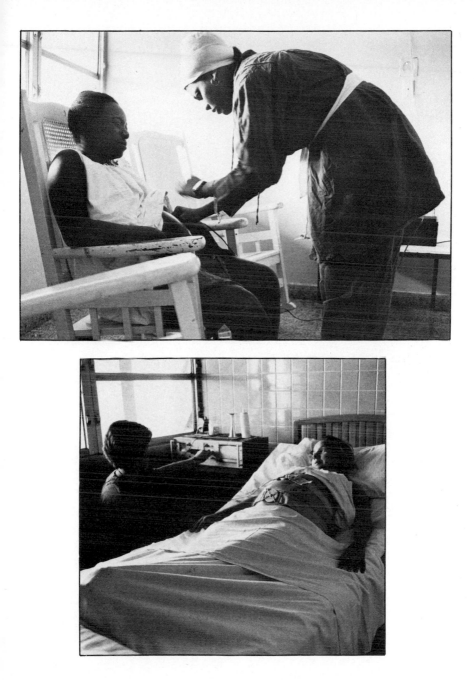

Top: Doctor gives routine prenatal care at Ramon Gonzalez Coro Obstetric and Gynecological Hospital, Havana.

Bottom: Monitoring the unborn infant's heartbeat at Ramon Gonzalez Coro Obstetric and Gynecological Hospital, Havana.

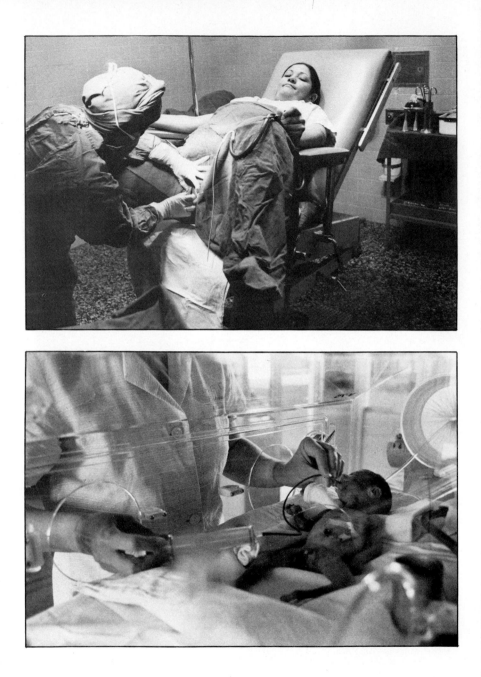

Top: Doctor examines patient in Argentinian Chair at Ramon Gonzalez Coro Obstetric and Gynecological Hospital, Havana.

Bottom: Four-day-old infant, born in its sixth month, being cared for at Ramon Gonzalez Coro Obstetric and Gynecological Hospital, Havana.

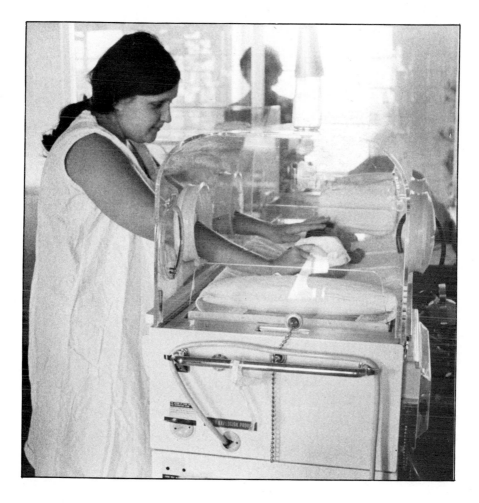

New mother touches her premature child for the first time, at Ramon Gonzalez Coro Obstetric and Gynecological Hospital, Havana.

Top: Infant care at naptime at the Sombreritos Mambíses Day Care Center, Aldabo.
Bottom: Sombreritos Mambíses Day Care Center, Aldabo.

Top: Dolls, Sombreritos Mambíses Day Care Center, Aldabo.
Bottom: Gardening at Sombreritos Mambíses Day Care Center, Aldabo.

Top: Biology students at the Lenin School, near Havana.
Bottom: Ballet students at the Cuba National Ballet Company School, Havana.

Top: Teaching biology at the Lenin School, near Havana.
Bottom: Physical education class held at the José Martí gymnasium, Havana.

Top: Havana student from the "13th of March" Junior High School gathers poles after the tobacco harvest. Near Güira de Melena.

Bottom: Work-study students from the "Batalla de Jigüe" Junior High School harvest potatoes. San Antonio de los Baños.

Visiting day at La Amada Tobacco Camp, near Güira de Melena.

Top: Students in art class at the Lenin School, near Havana.
Bottom: Chemistry experiment at the Lenin School, near Havana.

Dance students on a break at the Cuba National Ballet Company School, Havana.

Top: Peasant teachers harvest strawberries with work-study students from the "Batalla de Jigue" Junior High School. San Antonio de los Baños.

Bottom: Lenin School work-study students make athletic equipment. Near Havana.

Carmen Cantón: mother, worker, FMC leader, and economics student. Havana.

FMC poster on highway near Havana.

CHAPTER TWO

Peasant Women in a Changing Society

> *I'm over forty. I lived on the land that's now part of the*
> *Jibacoa Dam from 1955 to 1970, when I moved to the com-*
> *munity. We lived there the way all peasants lived before the*
> *revolution: very bad, no freedom, exploited. There was no*
> *electricity, no running water. The house was of boards, thatch,*
> *and a cement floor. And we weren't as bad off as most. My hus-*
> *band was a small farmer and I was a housewife. We decided to*
> *move because our land was needed to build the Jibacoa Dam.*
> *The Plan people came and discussed the problem with us. They*
> *explained that it was necessary, and we understood that it was*
> *important for the revolution, and so we moved to the com-*
> *munity. Before 1955, I had always lived in rural zones; mov-*
> *ing to the community was really a change in my life,* like
> leaping into the future.

Jacinta Odilia Orozco, peasant woman
and social worker at the Jibacoa rural
community.

Back in 1970, when I was working on my first book about
Cuban women, at one point I was up in a tiny village in the
Sierra Maestra foothills, a village called Buey Arriba, literally
upper oxen. Interviewing a peasant woman, thirty-eight-year-old
Haydée Méndez, I had asked her about her youngest child, and
she had told me:

> He goes to school up here, in Buey Arriba. You know the
> pride I feel when I see my three children? 'Cause I was thirteen

49

and I didn't know how to write yet, and I saw my son reading at the age of five! Today, any one of my kids knows more
than I do. . . .[1]

The differences between Haydée and her children made me
wonder what the differences must have been between her own
mother and herself. Haydée said:

> Ay, no, my poor mother! What a life of suffering that
> was! My mother had ten children, and did she work! My
> brothers and sisters and I never did go to school. The other day
> I was talking with someone and he said, ". . . When you were
> in school. . . ." And I told him, "Never in my life!" Later, as
> a woman, after my kids were grown, that's when I saw the
> inside of a schoolhouse for the first time. The little we knew
> we learned from my papa. My father taught his ten children
> how to read and write. . . . But we never saw a movie; we never
> could. That's the happiness my children have. We could never
> have had a scholarship. . . . Why, we didn't even hardly know
> what an automobile looked like![2]

Haydée's experience is typical of what peasant life was like
in Cuba before the revolution, especially in regard to women.
The difference between Haydée Méndez's mother's life and her
own was marked. The difference between her life and her children's would be more so.

Brief History of Cuban Peasantry and the Position
of Cuban Women

As in the case of native Americans in the United States,
Cuba's indigenous population conceived of land, air, sun, and
water as belonging to all who used them. The concept of private
property was introduced in Cuba with the Spanish conquest, when
great extensions of land were given to the conquerors. To work
the *haciendas*, the Spaniards quickly replaced the devastated and
decimated Indian population with African slaves. This was the
beginning of the latifundist system and the plantation economy.

[1] Margaret Randall, *Cuban Women Now* (Toronto: The Women's Press,
1974), p. 74.

[2] *Op. cit.*, p. 73.

Sugar, tobacco, and, later, coffee were the basic island crops from colonial times. Beginning in 1717, tobacco farmers in the Havana area rebeled against Spanish exploitation. Those were the first peasant revolts known in Cuba. Among the African slaves, in the seventeenth century, there was one sugar mill uprising after another. Eighteenth century slave rebellions were frequent, although short-lived, and not a few were led by women.

Today's strong Cuban woman clearly has her roots in protest and participation. There were determined fighters who, like Carlota at Matanzas' Triumvirate Mill,[3] risked everything for freedom. There were many women of Spanish descent who, in spite of their national origin, didn't hesitate to place their lives on the line for the consolidation of Cuban nationality and independence from Spain during the wars of independence.

The Cuban peasantry of Spanish origin was totally won over to the cause of the country's independence by the end of the War of 1868. When Carlos Manuel de Céspedes freed his slaves and called for the emancipation of blacks in Cuba, this vast sector of the population joined wholeheartedly in the struggle for freedom from Spain.

During the nineteenth century, the country fought for national independence. In the twentieth century, Cuban peasants were battling for land and against eviction, a common practice used by the large landholders against the small farmers who worked tiny plots. The Realengo 18 Movement against eviction from the land in the eastern mountain area was just one example of armed resistance by peasants in the 1930s. By that time, the old Cuban Communist Party (Partido Socialista Popular) had organized the sugar mill workers, and the working class-peasant alliance became the basis for future resistance.

Cuban peasantry made up large sectors of the *Mambi*[4] armies in the wars of 1868 and 1895. They again filled the ranks

---

[3] On November 5, 1843, a slave woman named Carlota led a rebellion at the Triumvirate Mill in Matanzas. The rebellion was crushed, and Carlota was killed. On November 5, 1975, the Central Committee of the Cuban Communist Party made the decision to answer Angola's call for troops. In honor of that courageous rebel, who may even have been brought to Cuba from the part of Africa which is now Angola, the Cubans called their participation in that country, "Operation Carlota."

[4] The native Cuban forces fighting against the Spaniards were called *Mambis*.

of the rebel army in the insurrection which brought a definitive revolution in 1959. In the early phases of that revolution, the fighters were mostly men, with some women, from the eastern mountain area. Peasant families were quick to provide a dependable rearguard supply line for the rebels. There are innumerable examples of women messengers, most of them peasants from the *sierra*. Women worked in the liberated zones, providing for the welfare of the troops. Women taught reading and writing to Cuba's largely illiterate peasantry, including many in the army. Women nursed and doctored in the campaign hospitals. More directly, at the battlefront, women were important contacts with the city underground, ran guns and ammunition (often from outside the country), and eventually fought in the Mariana Grajales platoon constituted in September 1958 shortly before the end of the war.

Culturally, the Cuban countryside was a conservative context for women in pre-revolutionary Cuba. The particular Spanish-African brand of sexism, which almost deifies women as a means of oppressing them, is deeply rooted in rural areas. Verena Martinez-Alier has explained in great detail the system of "carrying off" women in Cuba's rural regions during the nineteenth century.[5] As marriage was subject to equality of conditions in social class and lineage, young men in love made a frequent practice of "carrying off" women as the only means of consummating a union not likely to be socially acceptable. If the girl's parents refused permission for customary courtship because the man in question was too poor, did not have an adequate skill or profession, or was illegitimate or an orphan, the *rapto,* or "carrying off" process, settled all that in short order. Women were literally kidnapped, and their abductor subsequently reported same to the nearest officer of the law. Once she lost her virginity, the pairing that previously would have been a social taboo then became the only way of saving face or honor. This custom was not limited to the population of Spanish extraction; it was also practiced by those of African descent. Here, skin color was an additional factor: the lighter the skin of the man or woman, the

---

[5] For further discussion, see Verena Martinez-Alier, *Marriage, Class and Colour in Nineteenth-Century Cuba: A Study of Racial Attitudes and Sexual Values in a Slave Society* (Cambridge: Cambridge University Press, 1974).

better the chance of improving lineage and the more likely to obtain parental consent for the union. Lightness of skin color came to exemplify a social distance from slavery.

All this has left its mark on the Cuban peasant woman. In general, before the revolutionary victory, Cubans in the country-side were more racially homogenous than their sisters and brothers in the urban areas. The chaperone system was pervasive. This tight fabric of social and cultural conservatism, plus the real lack of educational and work possibilities for people as a whole and women in particular, led women to pair off at an extremely young age. In Cuba, even today, it is not unusual for women twelve, thirteen, and fourteen years old to marry and constitute a household, especially in the outlying areas.

Initial Revolutionary Changes

Before 1959, forty percent of Cuba's sugar, ninety percent of its electricity, fifty percent of its railroads, and twenty-three percent of its non-sugar industry were in the hands of U.S. monopolies. Under the prevailing colonial latifundist system in agriculture, according to the 1945 agricultural census, less than three percent of all existing farms occupied close to sixty-five percent of the total land. One million hectares (2.5 million acres) of fertile land were unused. Cuba's cane, the basis of the one-crop economy, was harvested by archaic methods, with resulting low productivity. In the extensive cattle-raising industry, insufficient genetic work yielded low milk productivity. The country's hydraulic works were in bad shape, there were few railway lines, and many areas were totally inaccessible.

In 1958, twenty percent was the officially admitted unemployment rate. Of every eight workers, only one was a woman, and that woman worked against all the disadvantages inherent in extremely limited job possibilities with discriminatory wages and virtually no benefits. Nearly one quarter of the country was illiterate, but the rate approached forty-five percent in the rural areas for the adult population, and it was even higher for peasant women. In rural Cuba, men averaged a third grade education and women much less. Many peasant women had never been to school at all; it was considered unnecessary since their futures were confined in any case to home and children.

According to the 1953 government census, more than half of the total Cuban population lived in sub-human conditions in which racial discrimination, vice, and prostitution flourished. People migrated from the countryside to the overcrowded city slums, as they still do all over Latin America today, in vain attempts to find work, food, and a future. Those most deeply affected by the country's economic and political situation were city slum dwellers and peasants relegated to remote areas where any kind of health care, education, or permanent work were simply unknown.

One of the first laws instituted by the victorious revolutionary government was a radical agrarian reform. During the war itself, in September of 1958, at the historic Congress of Peasants in Arms held in Mayarí Arriba, a provisional agrarian reform was implemented in the liberated zones. Raúl Castro and his army, on the second front, organized the peasants around rural health care, education, ownership of the land by those who worked it, and a war contribution of ten percent of crops sold.

Following liberation, the first Agrarian Reform Law for the country as a whole was passed on May 17, 1959. Through this first law, the large landholders, many of them foreign, were ousted, and the Cuban poor and moderate income peasants finally had a right to the land they had worked for generations. But sectors of the rural bourgeoisie who resisted the radical changes of a socialist revolution still had a foothold in the agricultural economy. A second Agrarian Reform Law was necessary, and, in October 1963, the law limited holdings to 67.7 hectares per person. This became the basis for the revolution's policy regarding this traditionally dispossessed class, bringing seventy percent of the country's land into the socialist sector of the economy and freeing 400,000 agricultural workers from semi-slavery.

Education

One of the mammoth tasks the new government took on was that of teaching the nation to read and write. As discussed earlier, the national illiteracy rate was 23.9 percent, rising rapidly in the rural areas and always much higher for women than for men. In 1961, Fidel called for an army of young people to go out into the most isolated areas to live with peasant families, each young man or woman teaching reading and writing to a group of illiterates while they lived in their homes, shared in the hard work of planting and harvesting, cattle-raising, wood-chopping, or whatever it was that the peasant family did to sustain itself.

That Fidel was able to convince the parents of 100,000 urban young boys *and girls* to allow their youngsters to go out and live in peasant homes for eight, nine, or ten months was an incredible feat, especially considering the high incidence of counterrevolutionary activity. As it was, bands of CIA-funded bandits tortured and murdered more than one brigadist. It was no coincidence that the Bay of Pigs invasion was perpetrated in April of that year, when many of the brigadists, preparing to ship out to their respective destinations, were bunked at that time very near the beach where the invaders came ashore. Several months later, Manuel Ascunce, a fifteen-year-old brigadist, and Pedro Lantigua, the seventy-five-year-old peasant man he was teaching to read and write, were captured by bandits, castrated, tortured to death, and strung up from the same tree as a warning to others involved in the giant task. Yet not a single parent demanded the return of a son or daughter.

Of course the new idea of universal education didn't end with the literacy campaign. Follow-up courses were immediate and varied. Schools went up everywhere. Almost anyone who knew a bit more than his or her neighbor was encouraged to make up for the giant deficit in teachers. "Those who don't know, learn; those who know, teach," became a slogan which continues to have meaning. Teachers went into the mountain areas, and many of those teachers who were women became the first rural organizers for the great mass organization, the Federation of Cuban Women.

Peasant women's lives, following the end of the war, were revolutionized. It wasn't possible to eradicate that much backwardness simply by installing one-room schoolhouses in the hills. There was too much catching up to be done, and it would be some time before adequate schools existed in all the rural regions. The Ana Betancourt School for Peasant Women [6] in Havana was to give these women a sixth-grade education, the beginning of a proletarian ideology, and specific skills. Among the skills, dressmaking was particularly useful. It was an activity culturally close to these women's lives. Who did not want to learn to sew for their families?

In 1961, following an FMC selection of women from the most remote areas of Oriente, Las Villas, and Pinar del Río, the first contingent of 14,000 women came to the Ana Betancourt program in Havana. The initial requisites were three: one had to be a peasant woman from an area where no adequate schooling yet existed, one had to be at least eight years old,[7] and one had to be willing to undertake this new experience. By 1963, the demand was so great that, at the end of each course, return tickets were given only to those students who really showed the desire and ability to stick with the educational process and put it to some use. At the end of 1964, 3,000 of these return tickets were issued. By the following year, the first graduates were in a position to staff the plan's new junior high school, and the women continued to increase their educational level. Each member of the first graduating class of 1,000 women back in 1961 had been given a sewing machine and was urged to teach ten other women from their area what they had learned. By the mid-sixties, the courses were much more comprehensive.

From the very beginning of the Ana Betancourt project, the idea of work and study, now typical of all Cuban middle and upper level schools, was very important. It was never a study program heavy in theory, and practice was always a vital complement to what was being taught. During the first semester of 1965, the best junior high school students studied half-time and taught fourth grade as well. The system led, in 1966, to the school's best graduates providing the teacher corps for the newly

[6] Ana Betancourt de Mora participated in Cuba's first War of Indepencence in 1868. In 1869, she stood up in the Guaimaro Constitutional Assembly and demanded women's rights. In 1974, at its Second Congress, the Federation of Cuban Women instituted the Ana Betancourt Medal, which is given to outstanding women throughout the world.

[7] In rural Cuba at that time, a girl was considered a "woman" at the age of eight!

created May First School for Peasant Girls, an outgrowth of the original plan, which eventually provided education for an enrollment of 20,000.

By 1966, many of the students displayed outstanding leadership capacities; the student organization at the schools was comparable to that in any city school. The following figures show the success of the program: in 1963, fifty-three percent of the students passed; this increased to sixty-eight percent in 1964; to eighty-three percent in 1965; and dropped slightly to seventy-nine percent by the end of the 1966 course. Since then, the promotion rate has climbed progressively higher, so that, in 1979, the plan keeps pace with the average Cuban school promotion rate which ranges from eighty to ninety percent or greater. Today, there are adequate educational facilities throughout the country, so that, while the Ana Betancourt School has kept its name in honor of its history, it is now a normal coeducational Cuban public school.

There were many other initial educational programs which, although not aimed at peasant women *per se*, did in fact affect and improve the lives of many of them. Among these were the special schools for domestic servants, where the maids of the bourgeoisie learned new skills and professions such as children's day care work, taxi driving, secretarial skills, accounting, translating and interpreting. Vast rehabilitation plans for prostitutes were established where the thousands of women formerly forced into this kind of life by capitalism could change their means of making a livelihood as well as gain the necessary self-pride through which their futures were radically altered. Other specialized schools drew upon students, in many cases from the aforementioned projects, for the first day care center child care workers and cooks, bank clerks, and taxi drivers. All of these programs incorporated many peasant women into the classroom and later into the labor force.

More recently, in the new rural communities, all kinds of classes are aimed at women improving their educational and cultural levels. Some women attend evening school on the stairwell landings of buildings being constructed in the newly-designed communities, so anxious are they to continue their education even before day care facilities permit using regular classrooms.

Apartment doors are left open, and the women can thus keep an eye or ear sensitive to sleeping children.

The National Association of Small Farmers

The National Association of Small Farmers (ANAP) was founded on May 17, 1961, to meet the needs for organization and unity among thousands of small farmers who had remained in Cuba, but who were not for the revolution, and some middle level peasants who vacillated in regard to the laws promulgated to achieve justice in the countryside. By 1979, the ANAP had a membership of more than 226,669 small farmers, of whom 157,404 owned their own land. ANAP had become a strong mass organization introducing new technology into agriculture, educating and raising the political and cultural levels of the peasants, organizing popular cultural activities, and representing the peasants in all phases of national life.

The ANAP and the Federation of Cuban Women jointly sponsor an institution called the FMC-ANAP Mutual Aid Brigades, made up of wives, sisters, and daughters of small farmers. These brigades have been essential in getting peasant women out of their traditional household role by involving them in voluntary labor. Such volunteer work not only prepares the women to enter the paid labor force but raises their ideological level and offers immeasurable help in assuring specific harvests — Pinar del Río tobacco and certain fruits and vegetables in different geographical areas.

The "Thesis on Peasant Women and the Role of the FMC," presented at the Federation's Second Congress in November of 1974, describes their work:

> The FMC-ANAP brigades were organized in 1966 with the main goal of contributing to the political and ideological development of peasant women while at the same time helping to resolve the need for labor in planting as well as harvesting crops at certain times of the year.
> The brigade has developed in a spirit of collectivity and the work accomplished is of political, economic and social importance.
> Our Second Congress will analyze ways in which we can

increase participation and productivity of peasant women in the different tasks at the grass roots level, to which end we propose

a) that we work to increase the participation of peasant women in the FMC-ANAP Mutual Aid Brigades,

b) that we guarantee that the brigade leaders attend the Leadership Council meetings at each peasant base and participate in drawing up the work plan there, and

c) that we establish a pay scale for brigade work, in line with current norms, the members of each brigade deciding if this work is to be paid individually or collectively.

Through these FMC-ANAP Mutual Aid Brigades, 100,000 women have moved beyond the limiting horizons of their individual homes and plots.

The New Communities

Cuba has a young population. From the estimated 1974 census of 9.2 million, thirty-seven percent of the Cuban people were under fifteen years of age, fifty-seven percent were between fifteen and sixty-four, with the remaining six percent over sixty-five. The yearly growth rate is 1.8 percent, predicting a population of approximately 11.2 million by 1985, and five times the current 9.2 million by the end of the century.

The growth rate in Cuba today is greatly influenced by the fact that infant mortality is down to twenty-three per thousand live births and life expectancy is up to seventy years. In 1953, fifty to sixty percent of the population in the cities was unemployed. By 1970 this figure was down to 0.6 percent. Residual unemployment was reduced even more in the following years, so that, by 1979, there is none to speak of.

This changing picture has greatly affected Cuban peasant women. Before the revolution, Cuba's peasant population lived mainly in arbitrarily organized and often isolated regions. The *bohío*, a palmwood shack with a palm-frond roof and most often with a dirt floor, could be found almost anywhere. People relied heavily upon a home economy much of the year. Access to services ran from difficult to nonexistent.

With the revolution, new housing became one of the priority

items. The worst city slums were the first to go, replaced by housing projects. There was building in the countryside, too, and many new villages came into being. These new villages brought new problems with them. Contradictions were produced by the transition from the age-old customs inherent in the lonely self-sufficient peasant life of years gone by to the post-revolutionary life styles necessitated by community dwelling in the new towns.

To deal with these problems, the Community Development Group was created in 1971. Nisia Agüero, head of the Group and National Coordinator of the Cuban Committee of Human Settlements, describes the initial stages of this project:

> . . . the villages built between 1959 and 1971, the year the Group came into existence, faced difficulties, and although it's true that a great many new dwellings had been built, it's no less true that many of the families occupying them brought with them the same old habits and problems that came from their life in isolated shacks. Since we knew this was true, we never thought a simple portrait of the situation enough. We knew what we'd find: the slightly lazy woman in her constant gossip with her neighbor, the apartments and the village as a whole somewhat dirty, uncared for, the kids not attending school regularly, and so forth. That's why the first phase of our work, in order to arrive at a satisfactory diagnosis there where they'd tell us they were going to build a new community, would be to carry out a sociological investigation before the buildings ever went up. We want to know all about each family, its social composition, its demographic characteristics, its values, traditions, the history of the area and of its inhabitants. Based on a knowledge of all these aspects, we are able to propose projects which make for a smoother assimilation of the change. And there's no question about this change in life style being enormous. Our job is to intervene so that it won't continue to simply be a physical change as it was from 1959 to 1971, but a profound social achievement that requires transitional adaptation. . . .[8]

Often the peasant is not eager to leave the land on which he or she has struggled for generations. Peasants are reluctant to make a move to the "unknown," when the obvious advantages

[8] Francisco Garzón Céspedes, *Un Teatro de Sus Protagonistas* (Havana: UNEAC, 1977).

may seem abstract. Peasant women have played a decisive role in encouraging this move. Women and children have been the first to want a change which will bring them closer to schools, hospitals, community centers, and other services.

In the "Thesis on Peasant Women and the Role of the FMC," the role of women in leading the family to make the transition from individual shack to community life is stressed:

> . . . We must emphasize as well the important participation of the peasant woman in the move to the new communities created by the Revolutionary Government as a result of the establishment of agricultural and livestock plans and waterworks.
>
> They have been a decisive factor, bringing consciousness to the nuclear family of the advantages to be had in these new villages, and once in the villages they continue to play an outstanding role.
>
> The peasant woman, conscious of her role in the construction of a new society, supports the revolution's policies with regard to the peasantry, and she looks for ways in which, as Fidel in his May 17, 1974, speech said, "we may encourage the principle of optimum use of the land in order to satisfy the needs of the whole population. In the future we must move to superior forms of labor and of production, especially in the country's basic crops."

Peasant Women in a Changing Society

The first big change in the life of a peasant woman was her incorporation into the FMC-ANAP Mutual Aid Brigades. Here, for the first time, a woman stopped working only for her husband or father. She moved beyond the limits of the home economy and took definitive steps toward economic emancipation. Although, in the beginning, work with these brigades was on a voluntary basis, work discipline was established. Later, the women began earning a salary.

At the Cuban Communist Party's First Congress, in December of 1975, two options for future development of Cuban rural areas were clearly outlined. One choice was the proletarianization of the peasant class through incorporation of individual plots of land into state farms. The second possibility was an intermediate step involving cooperatives, whereby peasants who cannot yet move to large agricultural plans with their new communities may elect to move their shacks closer together, finance social services through community profits, and become eligible for social security benefits (i.e., the Maternity Law, among others). This second option is known as the production cooperative. Theoretically, both options point toward the eventual disappearance of the peasant class, wherein men and women of the countryside become agricultural workers.

The dynamic of the cooperative movement is extraordinary. At the end of December 1977, there were less than 100 cooperatives across the country. By March 31 of the following year, there were 176, and only one month later, April 30, 1978, the number was 202. The average land area involved was 163 hectares per cooperative, and 32.5 percent of the cooperative member-workers were women. The 1979 figures show that two percent of the land which was formerly owned and worked individually is now in production cooperatives.

An analysis of women's participation in cooperatives is interesting. Women are members of the ANAP as well as men, but the ANAP has two kinds of membership: those who own land and those who fall into the category of socios or associates. The landowners are almost all men, while the vast majority of the associates are their wives and children. This follows not from any discriminatory law made by the ANAP itself, but from the previous traditional system of male property ownership. The few women landowners among ANAP members were likely to be widows who had inherited the land of their late husbands. With the new production cooperatives, this situation changes and the position of women is greatly enhanced.

By 1979, there were nearly 300 of the new rural communities throughout the island. Recent studies made of 180 of these new communities show that, in 1977, 38.8 percent of the women were incorporated into the labor force. This figure is considerably higher than that for women's labor force participation nationally for the same year. Since peasant women traditionally did not work outside the home, the facts present a very curious phenomenon.

According to a study done in 1975-76, only eighteen percent

of the women living in these communities worked. At that time, the figure was below the then 25.3 percent national statistic. Day care and other social services were made available to the women. The role of the community worker has been important in raising the necessary consciousness around the need to work. The new agricultural programs have plenty of attractive jobs for all who are willing and able to take them. By the following year, 1976-77, a group of livestock programs studied yielded the statistic of forty-four percent for women's labor force incorporation! As surprising as this seems, the livestock and cattle programs are precisely those with most job opportunities for women. A subsequent study of a group of sugar cane programs in Oriente, an area with few possibilities for women, showed a fifty-one percent women's incorporation!

Community workers are instrumental figures in the new rural towns. Every new community has one. They are almost all women who have usually grown up in the community itself even before the families moved to the new village. Party and other cadres in the area help to choose prospective candidates they feel are qualified to do well in this complex work. The new workers are then given elementary social work courses. The courses were first offered only in Havana; more recently, they have become available at the provincial level as well. The women then return to organize and manage many of the plans and projects and much of the responsibility for successful change falls upon their shoulders.

Another important agent for change in the new communities is the use made of people's theater. The Escambray Theater Group in the Escambray Mountains, in what used to be Las Villas Province, was the first to experiment with using theater as a means to deal with community problems among people in the countryside. A group of professional theater people, including some of the finest in the country, headed by Sergio Corrieri (known by American film audiences for his role in *Memories of Underdevelopment*), left their respective Havana theaters in 1970 and went into the Escambray area. They were looking for a way to bring their talents closer to the revolutionary experience. They felt that, at least at that point, theater lagged behind other art forms in terms of its relevance to the extraordinary social changes going on in the country. They chose the Escambray Mountains because specific factors made it a problem area. The last of the CIA-funded bandits were not routed out of the region until late 1965. A widespread petty bourgeois ideology had been inherited by great numbers of peasants with sizable acreage, and there was a strong interest in the region from an increasing population of Jehovah's Witnesses.

A first year of sociological investigation of the rural regions, with the assistance of the University of Havana and complete support both of the party and the mass organizations in the area, provided material for writing and adapting plays which would point to problems and possible solutions. By this time, the theater people had lived and worked with the peasant families, becoming a trusted part of the community. They began to put on plays from village to village, eliciting debates after each production. The local people quickly became involved in these discussions. After several years, the formal production-debate-discussion structure was no longer necessary. People directly interrupted performances—often contradicting the actors—if they thought something should be changed. A dynamic developed between the life of the theater and the life of the area, and a new consciousness gleaned from the theatrical experiences began to have its effect on the peasantry there.

The Escambray innovation, now almost a decade old, motivated other experiments with this kind of theater. Flora Lauten, from the original group, went to live in the peasant community called La Yaya, and there she began to work with local people. Her group's plays were produced and eventually even written not by professional theater people but by peasants who, perhaps ten years before, had never even seen theater, much less thought of participating in it. A theatrical movement was initiated which has now been extended throughout many of the rural communities. Nisia Agüero emphasizes its usefulness:

> As far as women's incorporation into the labor force is concerned, in spite of the fact that there are concrete problems—a lot of children and not all the social services yet resolved—the men, in many cases expressing a deeply-rooted sexism, don't want their wives out of the house. The La Yaya Theater Group has written plays like *This Mockingbird Has*

No Owner to discuss this problem. The Group doesn't only put the play on in La Yaya but goes also to other communities. . . .[9]

Jacinta Odilia Orozco, the community worker at Jibacoa, a new community in Havana province, talks about theater and consciousness-raising:

The theater has been essential in the development of the community. Just in terms of women's incorporation into the labor force, to give one example, theater has played an important role. At the beginning there were six women working in production here in Jibacoa. Today eighty-six percent of the women in this community are working. We owe this in great measure to the theater we have here. Our experience with the play about sexism was tremendous. We criticized the man who thinks his wife is a submissive object in the home, and we showed how women can't and mustn't accept that kind of attitude. We dramatized cases we have right here in order to debate them later with the audience, right in front of those directly affected. We always hold a debate after each performance because that's what makes people understand that the theater has an objective. What do you think of so-and-so who won't let his wife work? And the opinions begin: he's an egotist, he's wrong, the community was built so that everyone—men and women—can have the same opportunities. The revolution means full equality between men and women. . . .[10]

All these changes have, as one of their major goals, the breaking down of the differences between countryside and city. The peasant class is not going to disappear overnight, nor will any kind of coercion be used in this respect. The Cuban revolution has always been rigorous on the point that all decisions regarding the peasant's relationship to the land are based on considerations of locality, type of crop or livestock involved, and the will of the person concerned. Voluntary relocation is a sacred precept here. One has only to go into the Cuban countryside to see the tiny shack amid an immense regional rice or tobacco project, an example of the lone family not yet ready to move.

In this difficult, historically inevitable, but sensitive process of change, Cuban peasant women are emerging as a vanguard group, exemplary ideologically in terms of their adaptability and

[9] Céspedes, *Un Teatro de sus Protagonistas.*
[10] Céspedes, *Un Teatro de sus Protagonistas.*

creativity. Often, yesterday's child bride is today's community social worker, dealing no longer with her own frustrating or insoluble problems but with those of the entire collective: problems which today have a future solution that includes her own liberation as a woman.

CHAPTER THREE

Woman As Mother: The Right To Free and Complete Childbearing Attention

> *Woman is the natural workshop where life is formed. She is the extraordinary creator of the human being.*
>
> Fidel Castro

Small clusters of lonely crosses are scattered along Cuba's eastern coastline where the mountains slack off to the sea. It is said that the makeshift wooden markers are the graves of those who never reached a hospital, those who died along the way. Although these stories belong to a pre-revolutionary past, the crosses remain as bitter reminders.

Remote parts of mountainous rural Cuba often were accessible only by sea. Where roads existed, spring rains usually turned them to deep mud. Tax money wrung again and again from the people with promises of highways and hospitals more often than not ended up in the pockets of successions of dishonest government officials and regimes.

In those times, if a family got to a hospital or clinic with their human cargo still alive, another struggle awaited them. Only cash, which few peasants could muster, or the favor of a local politician, could get a person admitted. In 1958, there were only 28,536 hospital beds for close to seven million Cubans, and the vast majority of these beds were in the city. Except for middle and upper class women living in the larger cities, pregnancy and childbirth were simply "natural" occurrences to be coped with as well as possible on the dirt floor of a country shack or in an overcrowded slum.

The Decision: Having a Child or Not

In Cuba, from the onset of people's power, no state ideology regarding population control has ever been imposed on the people. Even though the country's population is not large enough to meet all labor needs, women have never been urged to have children by offering privileges or prizes for large families. On the other hand, although housing has been a major problem, large families have not been discouraged. It is the state policy, frequently articulated by Fidel Castro, that the size of the family is the decision of the husband and wife as part of their human rights. The state's duty is to provide the citizen with the means for having as few or as many children as they wish. Such non-interference is especially called for in a country such as Cuba, where there is clearly enough land to sustain a much larger population. Even if this were not true, socialism would seek to create a situation where economic considerations played no role in this most fundamental of human decisions.

The Cuban view is greatly influenced by the horrors of the population control schemes encouraged by the United States. Women in numerous developing nations have been forced or duped into sterilization programs. Often, they thought they were receiving temporary birth control measures or other medical treatment. In the Latin American world, Colombia, Peru, Bolivia, Nicaragua, Chile, and Puerto Rico have been victimized. In Puerto Rico, from 1959 to 1979, one-third of the women of childbearing age were sterilized. Even within the United States itself, minorities and the poor have been forced into sterilization by the linking of that operation to social services such as welfare. A program advertised as a concern for global survival clearly has been structured to promote economic ends with genocidal brutality. Cuba has turned away from any policy that even hints of population manipulation and posits that, under socialism, the planet could sustain a much larger global population.

Nevertheless, Cuba makes birth control information a free and standard service at all polyclinics. Intra-uterine devices and the pill are the forms of birth control most frequently prescribed. The pill was discouraged during the first years of the revolution because Cuban doctors felt the testing had been insufficient and the economic blockade made it extremely difficult to get adequate supplies from abroad in the necessary quantities. Now, Cuba manufactures its own birth control pills with low estrogen content. Diaphragms are commonly recommended, especially in rest periods between the use of one IUD and another. Condoms are available at all drug stores. Tubal ligation is performed in cases where it is seen as necessary to the woman's health, and then only after a thorough explanation has been given. A woman may request a tubal ligation as a solution to problems she considers determinate, such as age or having had as many children as she wants.

Abortions, provided they can be done in the first trimester, are readily available. They are free and carried out under the same hospital conditions as all other medical treatment. Standard procedure has been the D and C, but now vacuum aspiration is also widely used. After the first three months, an urgent medical reason for abortion is required. The national abortion rate in 1974 was 499 per 1,000 live births. The rate for Havana was approximately the same as that for New York City in the mid-seventies, even though there are obvious differences in accessibility, cost, and social attitudes.

The abortion issue, under capitalism, is critical for women, not because the right to abortion when needed is necessary for women's "control of their own bodies," but because without abortion rights females in the working class will not be able to struggle under equal conditions. Marian McDonald makes this point admirably:

> ... Marxist-Leninists know that abortion is only one ... of several childbearing rights that the working class and its allies ... must struggle for. ... Thus we begin by defending the right to bear children itself, to be free of abusive and genocidal sterilization. ... We fight for adequate pre- and

post-natal care, maternity facilities, and well-baby clinics, for
these are essential for the health of our community . . . we have
no illusions about capitalism's ability to deal with these concerns.
We know that only with socialism will we be able to create the
conditions for the full exercise of childbearing rights . . .[1]

In Cuba, where socialism has been fought for and won, some
of the most important immediate benefits have been reaped precisely in the area of maternity care.

From Before to After

To understand Cuba before the 1959 people's victory, one
has only to look at most other Latin American or underdeveloped
countries today. According to Inter-American Development Bank
figures, infant mortality "in nine Latin American countries ex-
ceeds eighty per thousand live births, and in two countries is in
excess of one hundred per thousand live births." Huberman and
Sweezy, in *Socialism in Cuba*, tell us that in no other Latin American country is infant mortality today less than forty-two per
1,000 live births. In the highly developed United States in 1977,
the infant mortality rate was seventeen per 1,000 live births according to World Health Organization statistics. One of the
health goals set by Cuba in 1974 was the reduction of the infant
mortality rate to twenty per 1,000 live births by the end of the
decade. In 1979, the rate had been lowered to 22.3 per 1,000
live births with continuous improvement expected to proceed
on schedule. In a parallel development, the mortality rate for
mothers was two per 10,000 deliveries, down from a rate of
5.6 per 1,000 deliveries only seven years earlier.
   In the years immediately following 1959, nation-wide health
programs began to have their first noticeable effect on lowering
infant mortality rates and improving conditions for pregnant
women and their offspring. The first health programs were not
directed specifically at these problems but at priority medical
areas where urgent attention was demanded. Indirectly, the results
of these medical policies affected maternity areas. For example,
previously Havana and a few other moderate-sized cities were

[1] Marian McDonald, "Radical Forum," *The Guardian*, 1978.

virtually the only places adequate medical attention was available, and there only for those who could afford it. When a rural health network was established, maternity concerns improved. Preventive medical attention aimed at widespread gastrointestinal infection was another far-reaching improvement. Medicine, in general, formerly of a curative nature only, became increasingly preventive and curative, with the emphasis on the former.

In the early years of the revolution, the system of information concerning health projects and their results was not as efficient as it might have been. In 1969, the continued decline of infant mortality was interrupted, calling forth new governmental actions. After a year of intensive study, a revised national maternity plan was put into effect. Among the major goals set for achievement before 1980 was the systematic reduction of the infant mortality rate to twenty per 1,000 live births,[2] of the first-year-of-life mortality rate to six per 1,000 live births, and of the mothers' mortality rate in childbirth to two per 10,000 live births. After the plan had been in operation for three years, the frequency of abortion was identified as another problem. More specifically, it was being used as an alternative to pregnancy. Without placing obstacles in the way of those who wanted abortions, health officials intensified work in the schools, homes, mass organizations, and media to spread information about birth control methods and where birth control devices could be obtained.

In line with these long-range goals, the Cuban Health Ministry set out at the beginning of the seventies to define the primary activities necessary to assure achieving their objectives within an already well-organized public health network. This, in turn, implied a series of short-range plans: to increase general health care and maternity attention in particular in all areas not yet up to the national standard; to carry out detailed fecundity studies in order to gain knowledge of potential demand for adequate available services; to study the incidence of miscarriage through hospital releases and a poll of the population at large; to broaden adequate family planning programs; and to improve existing services.

Such plans were based on four fundamental principles:

[2] This goal was met in 1979, when the infant mortality rate per 1,000 live births dropped to 19.3.

1. the people's health is the state's responsibility;
2. health services must be available for everyone;
3. the community must actively participate in all health programs; and
4. all health services are of an integral nature, that is, preventive and curative.[3]

Attention During Pregnancy

What happens in Cuba when a woman is pregnant and decides to have a child? If she has acquired a sufficient cultural level to be able to understand the importance of professional maternity attention, and the vast majority of Cuban women now fall into this category, she will probably go to the gynecologist at her local polyclinic. The polyclinic is the most local of Cuba's three medical facility levels.[4] Each clinic facility is prepared to serve approximately 20,000 persons in an urban neighborhood or rural area. The polyclinic provides the customary initial medical examination and begins the series of monthly and later twice-monthly visits and laboratory tests. At the same time, the pregnant woman receives largely preventive clinical care and also attends periodic talks given by doctors and other polyclinic specialists and personnel. Wherever possible, maternity care in special hospitals and clinics is separated from the treatment of illness, as childbearing is not considered a pathology.

During the first three months of pregnancy, the specialized talks cover the importance of adequate checkups, signs for early detection of possible miscarriage, sexual relations during pregnancy, diet, rest, and physical exercise. Discussions during the second three months cover maternity clothing and the importance of regular laboratory tests and exercise. Classes in natural childbirth also begin in this second trimester. If the local polyclinic has available space, classes will be held there; if not, the woman attends classes where she is expected to give birth. Expectant

[3] Unpublished paper presented to the author in 1978 by the administration of the Rámon Gonzáles Coro Maternity Hospital.

[4] Public health in Cuba involves the neighborhood polyclinic, the municipal hospital facility, and the larger and more complete hospital complexes with every possible specialty. Only three major hospitals in the entire country have separate maternity departments.

mothers, especially those giving birth for the first time, are actively encouraged to attend. Nation-wide, about seventy percent do, and, in Havana, the figure is from ninety-two to ninety-nine percent.

During the last three months of pregnancy, the periodic lectures cover the danger of premature delivery, the advantages of breast feeding, care of the newborn, signs of approaching delivery, advantages of hospital delivery, explanations of the different instruments and devices used in diagnosing specific problems related to the state of health of mother and child, and women's rights under the Maternity Law.

I have observed two different kinds of group sessions within the psychoprophylactic preparation carried out at the Ramón González Coro Maternity Hospital in the Vedado section of Havana: the weekly meeting of expectant mothers and fathers covering all phases of pregnancy, delivery, and child care held on Thursday evenings, and the weekly session with the women alone on Friday afternoons. Toward the end of the pregnancy, classes in exercises, relaxation, and breathing are held daily, and these two additional encounters are aimed at getting the participants to express any questions, uncertainties, or fears they may have. The meeting with the fathers involves a slide show followed by a discussion. A good cross-current of conversation was achieved, and the level of knowledge and interest the men showed in learning how to care for their children was impressive.

But the group dynamic with the women alone was far more intense. Some twenty-five women at different stages of pregnancy came variously from their homes or from the upper floors of the hospital where they were receiving special treatment of one kind or another. The women sat in a wide circle listening to the psychologist explain that they were there to discuss any question at all they might have, but that the session was not intended to be a question-and-answer one alone but rather the initiation of a collective conversation in which everyone should feel free to answer each other and to speak whenever they felt the need. The opening silence stretched out among hesitant, largely closed faces. Some eyes reflected concern, others made the rounds of sisters waiting for another to break the ice. When the talk finally began, it was torrential. A young peasant woman, claiming to have no problems at all herself, who almost sneered at the others' first half-formulated questions, turned out to be suffering real agony in understanding her ambivalence toward her coming child; it turned out that she had been upset because she had a mother who practiced witchcraft .The interaction among women of very different cultural and educational backgrounds was exciting and fruitful. Two and a half hours later saw real scientific information exchanged and clarified and an underlying solidarity among the women, which included the psychologist.

Women who live in remote mountain areas or other parts of the Cuban countryside where it is not so easy to make periodic visits to polyclinics or hospitals are encouraged to spend the last few weeks of their pregnancy living in special maternity homes run by the Federation of Cuban Women in conjunction with the Public Health Ministry. In 1979, there were sixty-three such homes with over 900 beds. These homes do not have an institutional quality or hospital atmosphere. Women at the maternity homes come together, reap the benefits of education sessions, and have their other late-pregnancy needs met. The homes frequently include day care services for women who must come accompanied by small children. The homes themselves are equipped to handle all childbirth needs.

However, if a pregnant woman is *not* aware of the importance of using these maternity services, she may be visited by volunteers who regularly canvass rural and urban neighborhoods where women still suffering from low cultural levels are likely to ignore the advantages of medical contact. House calls are made to encourage all pregnant women who might not automatically do so to begin their regular obstetrical visits early. Vitamins and any medication needed during pregnancy is free. Special milk and food rations are provided beginning with the fifth month of pregnancy and extending through the period of lactation.

The special rations are needed because, with the new distribution of the country's resources, *all* Cubans have equal access to food, clothing, and other necessary commodities. Underdevelopment and the twenty years of U.S. economic blockade have made temporary rationing necessary. Variety and quantity of goods change with increased production and trade. In the seventies, notable changes have taken place in the rationing of most items. Many — fish, eggs, yogurt, butter, fruits, and vegetables — have come off the ration book entirely. In 1979, every child in the country from birth to seven years of age was receiving a liter of fresh pasteurized milk daily. Pregnant and nursing mothers and persons over sixty-five also received a liter a day, while nuclear households of five or more members received a liter every other day. All future mothers in Cuba are issued coupons to buy other items necessary for their child's comfort. These include crib, playpen, plastic bathtub, diapers, and layettes. Women are encouraged to comply with the periodic polyclinic visits by the requirement that the coupons for infant goods be validated for use by the health center.

Special attention is paid to cases considered of a high obstetrical risk. In this category are women who have had problems in previous pregnancies, who have a history of certain kinds of complications in their families, who have laboratory tests showing danger signals of toxemia or other problems, and women expecting more than one child. These women are hospitalized depending on the particular situation for specified lengths of time determined by the category or by the specific case. Often they spend the greater part of their pregnancy in the hospital.

The overwhelming difference one may experience with health care in socialist Cuba as opposed to the United States, where medicine is extraordinarily advanced but unevenly distributed, is precisely the fact that in Cuba each new advance is made available to all. For instance, the ultrasound equipment now at the González Coro Hospital is a very recent medical technological development which can, in many instances, replace the dangerous use of x-rays. This scanning device transfers an image of the fetal cranium to a screen, making it possible to measure the diameter of the baby's head to obtain a fairly accurate estimate of fetal weight. This $20,000 machine is not used in isolated cases, but in every case where there is any discrepancy between calculated pregnancy time and the height of the uterus. The time and height information determines hospital admittance, special study, and consequent attention for women whose unborn babies are either larger or smaller than the supposed norm for that period in the pregnancy.

As of early 1979,[5] there were 116 maternity patient units in Cuba with more than ten beds each and, if smaller units are included, the total figure would be over 200. Only nine of the larger units were in the capital city; throughout the country, there were 7,280 obstetrical beds. Each local polyclinic served 9,800 women of childbearing age. Each of the almost 600 obstetrical consultation offices throughout the country, of which nearly 200 were in the rural areas, attended to approximately 3,300 women. There were more than 750 gynecological and obstetrical specialists in Cuba, or more than one for every 12,000 women. There were over 200 full-scale pediatric hospitals, or hospitals with pediatric wards, operating across the island. These pediatric units serviced 15,300 children apiece. There were over 9,000 pediatric beds, one for every thousand children, with a variance of from 0.9 to 1.2 among the provinces. Cuba's 1979 figures show that close to ninety-seven percent of all children were born under hospital conditions. Pregnancies averaged nine obstetrical visits each, with a variance of between 7.6 and 10.3 among the different provinces.

Emotional Health of Mother and Child

In an interview given in 1979, Isabel Delfino, the head of the psychology department of Havana's González Coro Maternity Hospital, explained how that institution attends the nonphysical side of the maternity experience. Classes are held for all pregnant women and their husbands, with attention directed to specialized services and research available to those who need them. The hospital has four psychologists on the staff as well as a psychiatric department.

The special lectures for pregnant women are based on the results of a study carried out at this hospital in which 340 women were polled about their basic concerns, each listing an average of four or five areas in which she had doubts. Some seventy-five percent mentioned nursing and general feeding as a concern, thirty-seven percent cited the baby's bath and physical hygiene,

[5] Background information obtained from conversations in 1978 with Dr. Enso Dueñas, Acting Director of the Ramón González Coro Maternity Hospital.

eighteen percent were concerned with handling the newborn, eleven percent were worried about how to avoid diarrhea and what to do if it occurred, and five percent had questions about the child's sleep pattern. A lecture, with audio-visual material was then prepared covering all these and other points. This lecture, given to all pregnant women attended by this hospital, has become the model for national use.

The lecture also identifies women with concerns beyond these basic child care questions. Women may have fears resulting from previous traumas, or they may not feel at ease with their doctors, or free to ask the kinds of questions to which they desperately need answers. A typical statement was, "I leave the doctor's office satisfied that I don't have high blood pressure and that my urine's all right, but I can never bring myself to ask the many other questions I have." Women around the world are all too familiar with the attitudes — a tendency toward paternalism, a condescending nature, and rushing the patient through — that make asking the other questions so difficult.

The Gonzáles Coro psychology department addresses itself to this situation by educating doctors and other personnel to the need for broadened psychological attention to pregnant women and by providing the answers to these concerns. Women who show anxiety are given a series of five weekly appointments with a psychologist. The issues the pregnant women disclose range from ambivalence toward the child's birth, to fears of not recovering her pre-pregnancy figure, dying at childbirth, having the child die, or of the baby being born with a malformation. Special attention is given to the woman's relationship with her mate, her family, and the society as a whole. Again, childbearing is seen as a normal psychophysical process, not as a pathology. The psychodynamics of false labor, for example, are accepted as a rehearsal needed by some women to be sure of what they will be facing when the real time comes.

The father's presence during deliveries is not usual in Cuba. Isabel Delfino explained that it is not discouraged, but in Cuba, when an idea is implemented, it is implemented for everyone. To encourage the father's participation in the delivery would mean large scale preparatory courses and many changes which hospitals do not have the facilities to carry out. But the greater participation of fathers is on the agenda for the future. Attention to the importance of the relationship between the mother and her child or children in the weeks immediately after delivery has done a great deal to reduce infant mortality. Cuba, shortly after the revolution, was the society imperialism accused of planning to ignore parental rights and to separate children from their families, and many confused parents actually fled or sent their sons and daughters out of the country, having believed these lies. The reality is that socialism develops the relationship between parents and children to a fuller dimension. Cuba puts human and scientific resources to work to improve conditions surrounding the crucial moments when new lives are formed.

Delivery

At the González Coro, I observed a group of women in various stages of labor on the hospital's third floor for labor and natural deliveries. Some women, for medical reasons, were confined to beds in the three or four-bed labor rooms, but most walked the halls or sat in rocking chairs, watching television or talking in a sunny sitting area at the far end of the hall. Nurses and other attendants were frequently in and out checking on intravenous medication, noting contraction times, or listening for the child's heartbeat on modern equipment specially made for that purpose. The relationship between hospital staff and expectant mothers was kindly, warm, and open. Perhaps the most impressive aspects were the lack of paternalism and the existence of mutual respect.

The women were aware of what was happening to them; *they were active protagonists rather than passive or frightened participants.* Women shared their knowledge to help each other, and they discussed, among themselves and with the doctors and staff, the different stages of labor, the baby's position, breathing, dilation, signs of approaching deivery, and what could be done to make things easier.

Each time a new shift of hospital personnel came on duty, every woman in labor was thoroughly checked by the new doctor on the floor, who compared these immediate observations with the information on the woman's chart. Dr. Hernández explained that the women came to this floor from one of two sources: either they were sent from another floor of the same hospital or they came from their homes to the hospital's emergency entrance, where a specialist on duty at all times admitted them and decided whether they should go directly to the labor rooms.

All medical personnel and visitors to the delivery room wear cap, mask, and cloth boots to cover shoes. So "dressed," in the delivery room, I found Elsa, one of the women Dr. Hernández had examined and prescribed medication for only a half hour before. Hermández and her three assistants scrubbed up and made Elsa as comfortanble as possible, instructing her to grab the two metal knobs on either side of the delivery table, to raise her head, and to push her chin into her chest with each contraction in order to bear down long and hard.

I could not help but compare this delivery with my own, one in New York City eighteen years ago and three more recently in Mexico, and with the many I myself officiated at as a midwife for several years in the Mexico City slums. The first thing I noticed was that Elsa's arms and legs were not tied down to the table. She was totally free to move about and seemed to have sufficient preparation to keep calm and follow instructions well, in spite of complaining, after a long labor, that she was exhausted and could not push any harder. Later, talking to the hospital's director, Dr. Enso Dueñas, I learned that this method has been the standard procedure throughout the country for some time. Very, very rarely do Cuban deliveries involve the use of anesthesia or pain-killers.

Cuba is experimenting nationally with the seated position for childbirth. This hospital, like many others, has an Argentinian delivery chair in one of its delivery rooms, as well as the more conventional table in another room for prone expulsion. The director of the hospital explained that they are completing an in-depth study that compares both methods and, to this effect, in normal deliveries the methods are alternated with expectant mothers previously prepared for either. Although modern studies on seated childbirth date to 1886, when the French doctor Paul Rodet discussed its use among primitive peoples, in Cuba it wasn't until 1950 that Doctors C. Alvarez Lajonchere and Pedro Castro renewed interest in this methodological change in child-bearing. The revolutionary victory has made broad-based investigation possible. Dr. Lajonchere insists that "The horizontal position affects the woman psychologically because it propitiates passivity; it is necessary that the woman actively participate in the birth of her child, and this must be the focal point of our psychoprophylactic guidance."

At the particular childbirth I witnessed, the atmosphere was relaxed and efficient in a delivery room in which from three to four hundred babies are born monthly. The woman on the table, now imminently ready to deliver, had forgotten she was "too tired to push" and was fully involved in the birth of her child. A very moderate episiotomy was called for. The baby, an eight-pound-one-ounce boy, made his appearance seconds later. The doctor was telling the mother that "it's a boy" and the mother was telling the doctor that "that makes two," as I followed the baby out to observe the procedures used for phlegm removal, care of eyes, checking of respiration, and weighing and measuring.

While the mother was helped from the delivery table to a mobile stretcher to be taken to the post-delivery room, everyone shared in her joy with a few words of congratulations or a smile. We squeezed each other's hands as the stretcher rolled past where I was already removing my cotton boots, and our eyes met in silent laughter.

At the González Coro, as well as in all other maternity installations throughout the country, stays for normal deliveries run between three and four days after birth and, for caesarean sections, the time is usually six to seven days. A mother whose child must receive more hospitalization is free to remain with her infant for as long as necessary.

The Immature or Premature Baby

On the seventh floor of the González Coro is a special care wing. Behind glass partitions, sealing the viewer from what's going on in the sterilized area beyond, another important part of the maternity care world exists. This is where premature in-

fants or others requiring special attention are cared for by a
specially trained staff of doctors, nurses, technicians, and attendants. The most modern incubators house human beings so tiny
and fragile that one has difficulty imagining their survival. Some
clearly have more complex problems, and are being mechanically
aided in their breathing; others are being fed intravenously.

Similar special care units undoubtedly exist in major hospitals
throughout the world, but there are two important differences.
First, in a country such as Cuba, this service, which means life
as opposed to death for children requiring this kind of attention,
is absolutely free and available to everyone. Secondly, the mother
of these children are not on our side of the glass looking anxiously
and helplessly in at their problem offspring, but are sitting in
rocking chairs beside the incubators, talking to the new babies,
learning from skilled personnel how to manipulate the infants
through the incubator in-sleeves, rejecting traditional obstacles
as they develop the mother-child relationship so important, ultimately, for both of them. The vast majority of immature or premature infants graduate from the primary incubator section of
this special care unit to the nonincubator section where their
mothers can enter into a more intimate relationship with them.
This whole emphasis on the care of "premies" and babies with
birth deficiencies has been one of the main factors in reducing
Cuban infant mortality.

There are also babies in this section, however, that cannot
be saved. Isabel Delfino describes one such case where the baby
wasn't expected to live more than a few weeks. In cases of extreme deformity, an attempt is made to counsel the mother not
to view her child and, where death is certain, a relationship is
discouraged. But, in this case, the mother insisted on her right
to care for her child until it died, and she was judged psychologically capable of doing so. Her request was granted, and she
moved with him to the special care unit. She helped with his
care throughout his week-long life. Isabel expounded on the
fact that this woman's trauma was minimized, and her adjust-
ment to what had happened as well as her attitude toward becoming pregnant again were influenced in a very positive way,
by the fact that not only was she convinced everything possible
had been done for her offspring, but by her own experience of

participation, which had been crucial to her capacity to assimilate the tragedy. It is one thing for a woman to receive the news of her baby's death from her doctor or someone else in the removed atmosphere of her room or ward. It is quite another for the events to be part of her own personal experience.

The Milk Bank

In Cuba, everything is done to make nursing feasible and easy. Talks on the advantages of nursing are part of a woman's pre-natal education. Cuban doctors believe that the remarkable upswing in infant health is at least partially due to widespread nursing. New mothers are encouraged to nurse whenever the baby seems hungry during the first few days of its life; the baby itself will regulate its schedule. Women are taught how to care for their breasts and nipples during and after pregnancy. Later, working mothers are granted time off with pay in order to nurse. A most interesting aspect of this part of the mother-infant relationship is the milk bank that exists in all Cuban maternity hospitals. Every morning, an attendant with her streamlined milk cart and electric extraction apparatus makes the rounds of the hospital rooms where mothers are already rooming-in with their newborn. Women with abundant milk donate what they don't need for their own offspring, and all healthy mothers may, if they wish, give a little just to stimulate their flow. This milk stock is then sterilized and given to babies whose mothers are unable to nurse. Frequently, mothers with unusually large amounts of milk voluntarily contribute milk some time after they leave the hospital in a gesture of solidarity with infants and mothers. This system assures *all* infants of this unequaled natural immunity and well-being.

The Working Woman's Maternity Law

Maternity leave was established in Cuba in 1934, and it supposedly benefited all working mothers-to-be. However, it failed to meet the needs of the great majority of these women.

Since its benefits did not cover peasant women, or the thousands of prostitutes, or the great numbers of maids and women who did the multiple odd jobs in the bourgeois society, on March 27, 1963, maternity leave was included in the general social security legislation under the following clauses:

1) maternity benefits were extended to all working mothers-to-be in both the state and private sectors;

2) a twelve-week pre- and post-natal paid leave of absence was guaranteed;

3) every working mother was granted one hour a day, without having her pay docked, in order to nurse and care for her baby;

4) pregnant women who worked received services and material items necessary to their pregnancy and the well-being of their children up to the time of release from the maternity hospital; and

5) a cash subsidy was granted to working mothers whose babies were born in private hospitals (which still existed at that time in Cuba).[6]

These 1963 clauses were certainly an improvement over existing benefits. But by 1974, the revolution had consolidated a social and economic base sufficient to underwrite wider benefits. Law #1263 went into effect on January 14 of that year. Among other things, the new law:

1) increased the benefits of maternity leave in recognition of women's contribution to the construction of a socialist society;

2) guaranteed medical care during pregnancy, childbirth, and the post-natal period;

3) guaranteed medical care for the mother and the newborn child;

4) extended the period of paid maternity leave to eighteen

[6] The Cuban Maternity Law appears in *La Mujer y el Socialismo en Cuba* published by the Cuban government. See Appendixes III and IV for a reprint of The Working Woman Maternity Law and its Regulations.

weeks, twelve of them after birth (in case of a multiple pregnancy or error in calculating the date of birth, this period may be extended another two weeks); and

5) guaranteed an additional non-paid leave of absence of up to one year for those mothers who cannot return to work because their children require special care (in these cases, the woman's same position and pay will be waiting for her on her return to work).[7]

Part of my preparation for this essay was an intense period of observation and study at the Gonzáles Coro Maternity Hospital. Throughout the experience, I noted my questions, and, on the last day, I met with Dr. Dueñas as well as several of the department heads for answers. When I told them how moved I had been by different aspects of the hospital attention and the kind of human relations I had seen, Dr. Dueñas cautioned me, as he had before, about portraying too glowing a picture of Cuban maternity care. "We are still an underdeveloped country," he insisted, "a country that has suffered and continues to suffer from an economic blockade."

To be sure, there are still many things Cubans don't have. But maternity care, like medical attention in general, is based on totally different principles from the ones which existed prior to the revolution. One may find a doctor with a poor sense of a patient's psychological needs, or one might run across a doctor who is rude or irritable toward the person being treated, but one won't find a doctor whose relationship with the patient is based on the cost of consultation or treatment. The premises are completely different: health services are now based on the people's right to have them and the state's obligation to provide them.

---

[7] *La Mujer y el Socialismo en Cuba.*

CHAPTER FOUR

Development of the Family

There was a pain there, the pain of hearing Tassende—
Jose Luis—saying: "I always loved my daughter, I didn't abandon
her, I came here because I love her." He wasn't sure his daughter
would understand that, and he said it over and over again.
We heard other comrades saying: "Maybe my mother thinks
I don't love her because I'm causing her this pain and maybe
I love her more now than I've ever loved her...." We went
to Moncada with the same passion with which we go to cut
sugar cane today, the same passion with which we see our
schools filled with girls and boys from the countryside. Be-
cause when we went to Moncada we lived all this in our
heads. We didn't know if we'd live to see it, but we were sure
it would come about. And that's why we went in search of
life, and not of death.

> Haydée Santamaría, speaking about Moncada,
> July 13, 1967

It's almost seven in the evening. Your eyes ache from reading
galleys of six and eight-point type all day. You work in the
History Section of the Social Sciences publishing house, and,
after six years as a secretary there, you decided to take a course
in copyediting. Soon after completing the course, you've been
moved up to proofreader and style corrector. It's almost seven,
and you have to rush to make it to the day care center on time
and get home with your youngster in time to eat, share the day's
events with your husband and older children, and get to the FMC

meeting. Tonight's meeting is important because it's the election of outstanding women from this past three-month period.

On the way to the day care center, you remember that someone at work today told you about some great fried rice they're selling on 17th and 12th Streets. You detour two blocks, silently cursing the inadequacies of the rush hour transportation, you buy five portions, empty them into the plastic bag you always have folded in your purse for occasions such as this, and hurry to pick up your daughter just as the last mothers and fathers dash off with their little ones. It's only six blocks to your apartment, a new high-rise built with microbrigade labor[1] and awarded through your husband's workplace last year. He's a lathe operator at a furniture factory. You can hear your son's voice and your husband shouting something to your middle daughter as you run up the stairs.

José has been home for an hour or so and he's got dinner almost on the table. The two oldest are tidying up the living room in their typical makeshift way. Your husband has gone to a little extra trouble, after stopping at the grocery store, and you can smell his specialty — fried eggplant in tomato sauce. It will go well with the rice, you think, as you give him a hug and empty the still warm contents of your plastic bag onto a large platter. Your son is relieved that dinner is finally ready; he wants to get to the baseball stadium early. Las Villas is playing Havana, and the stadium is always packed, especially since people's CDR voluntary labor turned it into the biggest and best in Latin America, and since, with the revolution, all sporting events are free.

[1] Microbrigades are teams of voluntary construction workers going out from work places to build apartment houses with government-supplied materials. Workers involved agree to leave for approximately nine months to build, typically, a four-story, twenty-apartment unit. Their co-workers must also agree to keep production levels up in their absence. Once the finished building is checked by the Buildings Ministry and all the apartments are furnished, it reverts back to the workplace. There the workers elect a committee from among their own ranks to evaluate workers' bids for new housing. This committee investigates people's needs, brings its suggestions to a mass meeting, and the final say lies with the workers as a whole. As of September 1973, the date of the Chilean coup, one apartment from every new building is given to a Chilean refugee family; the other nineteen go to people from the workplace. Rent is six percent of one's salary. In this way, Cuba is attempting to solve its still critical housing problem. Tens of thousands of microbrigade buildings have gone up across the country.

Cari, your fourteen-year-old, has just joined the Federation, so she'll be going with you to tonight's meeting. Your husband has to go to school. He's going to college on the worker-student night school plan. You will leave the apartment door open because the FMC meeting is held on the stairwell, and, this way, you will be able to hear your four-year-old's cries if she awakes. . . . Two hours have passed. It was a good meeting, with a lot of discussion. You meet José as you approach the apartment door from different directions. He did better than he thought he would on a history test, so he's feeling good. You are both exhausted as you get into bed. Before you fall asleep, you think about the manuscript you want to discuss with your section head tomorrow, and you feel José's fingertips on your shoulder. . . .

The foregoing might have been a slice of life from any city-dwelling Cuban woman in 1978. A family life similar and yet very different from what it would have been twenty years ago. How have these changes come about? How has the Cuban socialist revolution affected the institution of the family?

Families and Exile

The revolutionary victory of January 1, 1959, brought fundamental changes to Cuban life. National resources, communications, transportation, banks, and services were quickly nationalized. A profound agrarian reform gave the land to those who worked it. Urban reform laws did away with exploitation through exorbitant rents and distributed existing housing on a much more equitable basis. New housing began to eradicate the worst slum areas such as Las Yaguas in Havana. People's basic needs for health care and education became everyone's right — and free. With their destinies for the first time in their own hands, the Cuban people began the long and difficult task of building a socialist state on the ashes of fifty years of imperialist domination and centuries of Spanish colonial rule.

The revolution inherited underdevelopment, a national consumerist mentality, a popular dream of the "American Way of Life," endemic parasitism and other poverty-produced diseases, and a toll of 20,000 war dead. In addition, its U.S. neighbor didn't take kindly to the idea of a country rebeling so close to home, and military and economic reprisals were immediately forthcoming. The United States didn't stop at attempting a full-fledged military invasion (Bay of Pigs) or an economic blockade (still in effect); it also used subtler methods. At the height of the cold war period, an intense anticommunist campaign was easily launched.

It wasn't long before carefully designed rumors, called *bolas* in Cuba, invaded the island: "The government is going to take your children away and send them to the Soviet Union!" "Communism means loss of parental rights. . . ." "The communists are going to close the churches!" "Everyone's going to be militarized." The Cuban family was a tightly-knit group. Traditionally, several generations shared a household. Grandparents, parents, and children were interdependent and emotionally close. Spanish custom was especially prevalent among the petty bourgeoisie. Young girls and unmarried women didn't go out without a chaperone, mothers were over-protective of both sons and daughters (but daughters most of all), and husbands' and fathers' words were law.

The demands of the revolutionary society changed all that. Women who had participated in the insurrectional struggle or who had been won over by the first important reforms — women, in short, who understood that the new power was *their* power — defended *their class interests* by becoming involved in the dozens of jobs that had to be done. They joined the Federation of Cuban Women; they joined the militia. They built schools with their own hands and sent their sons and daughters to the year-long literacy campaign in 1961. This meant that women no longer stayed home while their husbands were "out with the boys" or "working late." Their lives began to take on a meaning they had never had before, and this, naturally, brought clashes and struggles in more than a few family units.

The oligarchy left the country in droves. A goodly portion of the petty bourgeoisie left as well. They lacked a larger vision and saw their individual interests threatened, so they joined an exodus which, as of 1980, was estimated at a million people (out of a 1959 population of barely seven million). Some parents, who had indicated a desire to leave the country but whose departure date hadn't yet come up, panicked because they believed the *patria potestad*[2] rumors. They sent their children ahead; they would follow later, or, in some cases, because of extenuating circumstances, never did leave. There was a period when people were departing at the rate of some 200 a day.

In this way, many Cuban families were affected by the social upheaval. Almost every family, at least among the middle class and in the large urban areas, had an aunt, a cousin, a father, a sister, or a brother who left. The Cuban family, often in very complex ways, became deeply involved in the class struggle. Blood was no longer thicker than water. In isolated cases, but enough so that they deserve mention, brothers and sisters or fathers and sons actually found themselves on opposite combat sides. This happened at the Bay of Pigs and in the Escambray Mountains, where the U.S. CIA encouraged and supported groups of counterrevolutionaries who were not completely defeated until the mid-sixties.

This was not the norm, but the case of immediate family members on either side of the Florida straits was. People went to the United States, or sent their children, with Hollywoodian dreams. They often experienced the culture shock of a strange country where they stopped being completely Cuban and never really became fully American. They encountered anti-Latin racism, the alienation of a highly industrialized society, and the corruption and demoralization of the exile community in Miami and New York. There are stories of young women from protective petty bourgeois backgrounds who became maids in Tampa or Gainesville. The children grew up in the drug-laced, fast-moving, Vietnamized sixties, and not all of them retained their parents' ideology. What radicalized youth in general in the States in those years also radicalized many of these transplanted Cuban youth.

Gradually, groups of young Cuban exiles, people who had been six or eight or nine years old when their parents sent or took them from their homeland, began to get together and question their reality, the "American Way of Life," and what they had been told about the Cuban revolution. Some of these young

---

[2] *Patria potestad* is judicial control over one's children until they come of age. While rumored to be a law, no such legislation ever existed.

people started a magazine called *Areito*. They were instrumental, finally, in organizing the first Antonio Maceo Brigade. Members of the Brigade consisted of Cubans who left or were taken from Cuba before they turned eighteen and who had begun to believe that lifting the economic blockade and better relations between Cuba and the United States could only benefit all concerned. These young adults were curious to see for themselves what had really happened in Cuba. The first brigade visited and worked on the island for three weeks in 1977. The experience was a revelation. Especially intense and moving were the encounters between the exiled Cuban youth and family members they had left behind. In some cases, this meant a son or daughter being reunited with parents.

A typical case was that of Jorge Cañas. His parents had sent him to the States when he was thirteen, planning to follow soon afterwards. When his older brother came of military age, and was drafted, his parents forestalled their trip. One thing led to another, and they never left. Cañas, on the first Antonio Maceo Brigade, recounts his family meeting reunion:

> ... I remembered the streets and they felt familiar as we approached my house. Nevertheless, the exact moment of our arrival, when we parked the car, was unexpected. All of a sudden I found myself in the middle of a large group of people— thirty or forty, people of all ages. The car stopped, the door wouldn't open and I couldn't even get out. Some little boys around eight or nine years old helped, and they were the first to shake my hand. I see lots of faces I don't know and people hug me as I move from one to another. Suddenly, a woman stands out from the rest and she comes toward me with her arms open. I hesitate. It's my mother. ... As we hug my father appears to one side and my older brother to the other. The aunts and uncles, cousins, friends, neighbors: more hugs and greetings. We go in through the garden, I see the pine tree I planted sixteen years ago when it was two feet high. Now it's this tree that's taller than the house. The living room is just like I remember. They bring me a cold beer and I really begin to stop feeling like I'm watching a movie and become the protagonist of the most important experience in my life.

> Meeting with my family again was very meaningful for me and I can only compare it to the reencounter with my country. I had left Cuba in 1962 at the age of thirteen, alone,

sent out by my parents because they were victims of the fears, primarily sown by the United States, that they were going to take *patria potestad* from the parents and send their children to the Soviet Union. I spent my adolescence mainly in Catholic social service homes, until I was seventeen and went off on my own. The return to my country was the culmination of a whole process of searching for my identity and my roots that involved many different roads and difficulties. It's been the most significant experience of my life, up to now, and as such it's replaced the experience which had previously occupied that place: my departure from Cuba. . . .[3]

In the United States, the Cuban exiles tried to stop history, suffered alienation, isolation, and culture shock — to say nothing of exploitation, racist assault, and, in many cases, the realization that they shouldn't have left. Meanwhile, in Cuba, the family also suffered the jolts of human wrenching and tearing, but they suffered and grew in a very different context.

As people begin to realize what it means to actually hold and control their collective destiny, all sorts of things begin to happen. A new kind of freedom is born. Women are no longer faced with either submission to dominating husbands and staying in the home or assertion of their *individual* human rights to move beyond the home arena in defiance of their husbands. Now, there was a third choice: along with hundreds of thousands of other women and men, they could move beyond their limited horizons to attend meetings, join the militia, do volunteer work, or enter the paid labor force. And they did.

The revolution itself quickly broke down over-protective parent-child relationships. The literacy campaign of 1961 was the first large scale experience of this kind. After the literacy campaign, there was the giant coffee harvest (1962) and the rescue teams in the wake of Hurricane "Flora" (1963). There were the young art instructors who went into the countryside offering culture to the people, the Centennial Youth Column, the Youth Work Army, and, in 1978, 732 young Cuban teachers who went to Angola.

The relatives who left Cuba bombarded families who stayed with letters filled with stories of ranch-style split-level duplexes

[3] From *AREITO*, special issue on the first Maceo Brigade trip.

and pink refrigerators. Some actually enjoyed these "luxuries"; others had themselves photographed in front of houses they had never set foot in because they felt they had to justify their decision to leave. In Cuba, the first ten years of the new process were particularly difficult, and sacrifices were a necessary part of every day. Rationing was equitable but strict. But people experienced a kind of joy impossible to equate with either real or imagined packed freezers.

The new consciousness developing among young people, faced with parents or friends who left, is reflected in innumerable stories, films, songs, letters, and poems. The following three poems in particular deal with the problem. The first, "Not to Ever be Spoken of with my Mother," is by José Yanes. In an imaginary conversation with his mother, Yanes says:

Mom:
If José Martí
had never written anything at all
(not even to Mercado).
If he'd never dragged his hunger
and the soles of his shoes across America.
If he'd died of a common cold.

If Benny Moré
had never come into this world,
if he'd never come out
with *Santa Isabela de las Lajas.*

If I hadn't learned philosophy
from the park in Marianao,
if my ears had never learned
that you could swing with the *tibiri-tabara.*
If no one ever told me:
—Nague, I'm the most!

If people couldn't talk
without saying a word in this country
and everywhere else wasn't nowhere.

If Fidel hadn't blasted us
with *History Will Absolve Me,*
and he hadn't gone into the mountains
and there weren't any scholarship students
and we didn't speak of dialectics

and Marxism,
if our hunger was our fault
maybe I'd say o.k.
and make this trip with you
(and there are still the palm trees
and the sun and green forever).
This trip that's not even yours,
doesn't matter to you,
belongs to your daughter-in-law, to my brothers,
that you didn't think up
yet you bear up under
'cause you know they won't be able
to earn their bread.
Because your problem, mom,
is always how to find a new problem.
Now that you no longer had to stand for
my drunken father
calling your dead mother names
(remember how we had to leave the house).

If things were the way they aren't
I'd go with you,
if only because of these memories I have
of my belly aches
that went away
when I'd see you coming
with that little fingernail kit,
'cause dad wouldn't give you a cent.
So you wouldn't leave surprised
that I didn't want to go to work
in the cannery
and then discovered me
covering bits of paper
with ideas about love and humanity.

If things weren't the way they are
I'd go with you
to keep you from crying in the night.

If Lezama could make you understand
that the family, once formed, disperses
and you decided you're not going anywhere
and lived out your years for yourself,
you wouldn't have to wear yourself out
thinking of how you're going to make it
in that strange country,
you know nothing about,

beginning again at forty-plus.
If that's the way things were,
I wouldn't be crying on this bench
in this park
the tears wouldn't be running down my cheeks.
Because it's not just a matter
of the family leaving
and so what:
it's hell, mom.[4]

In the second poem, Victor Casaus speaks to a friend who's
been gone ten years:

BARBARA

You're of a world I hated
against which I'd have flung the best of my hatchets
or spit
          but in the end
          we found each other
at Martí's Monument 1960 to talk
to convince you with my poor arguments
don't leave the country
Barbara don't tell me your father
please
the way we live
I looked at you I looked at your breasts above all
trembling
in the night air
your strong legs tremendous I thought
and spewed phrases
from some book I don't remember
Martí? Or history?

---

[4] Ernesto Cardenal, *Poesía Cubana* (Mexico, D.F.: Editorial Extemporaneos, 1977).

The poem is so intimately Cuban that it needs some explaining of words and terms. José Martí was writing a letter to Manuel Mercado the night before he was killed at Dos Ríos; the letter remained unfinished. Benny Moré was a popular Cuban singer in the forties and *Santa Isabela de las Lajas* one of his best-known songs. *Tibiri-tabara* was a popular tongue-twister in the late fifties and early sixties, and *Nague* is the equivalent of "Hey, nigger!" used by one black talking to another. *History Will Absolve Me* is the defense speech Fidel Castro made at his trial after the Moncada Barracks attack in 1953. Lezama refers to José Lezama Lima, an important Cuban poet who was also a friend and mentor to Yanes.

Those who left before you did
we don't hear much about them
two professors living suspiciously together
in Pittsburgh
the school masters living well in Ohio of course
I don't know:
no news about you at all
By now you'd be like me over twenty I remember you
now that we're coming to the end of the decade
each on our own side
This thing that pissed your parents so
is ten years old
We're in the middle of a long year
your parents wouldn't have understood that either
There at Martí's Monument where we talked 1960 Barbara
now I'd have fewer pat phrases more real things
to tell you
I'm singing an anthem you wouldn't understand
God bless your breasts wherever they are
too bad they didn't choose to tremble in History.[5]

The "long year" Casaus mentions is the eighteen-month giant sugar cane harvest of 1969-70. In both these poems, José Martí is used as a symbol of Cuban identity, revitalized in and through the current revolutionary process.

The third selection is a short poem by Miguel Barnet called, simply, "Revolution":

When the revolution came
multitudes entered my house
They seemed to be going through drawers,
closets, changing the sewing basket around

That old silence was no more
and my grandmother stopped weaving memories
stopped speaking
stopped singing

Hopeful I saw, I had to see,
how the light came into that room
when my mother opened the windows
for the first time.[6]

[5] Victor Casaus, *Entre Nosotros* (Havana: UNEAC, 1977).
[6] Miguel Barnet, *La Sagrada Familia* (Havana: Casa de las Americas, 1967).

In October of 1978, at the Cuban revolutionary government's invitation, a broad representation from the Cuban exile community traveled to the island to take part in a historic dialogue. The government representatives and the representatives of the exiles spoke of everything: prisoners still serving time for crimes against the people, families that had been separated for up to twenty years, the very national identity of Cubans living outside the country. The government agreed to release the vast majority of political prisoners, at the rate of 400 a month, dependent on the U.S. acceptance of those who, on release from prison, wanted to leave Cuba, which was only about twenty-five percent of those leaving jail. Ex-political prisoners whose circles of family and friends lived outside the country and who wished to join them were also free to go, although the U.S., for one, has shown less willingness to accept these people. Cubans living outside the country, who had not been involved in terrorist activity against the revolution, were permitted to return to visit after January 1979. A country could only take such steps from a position of extraordinary strength and sensibility. The Cuban decision inalterably polarized the exile community, further isolating the remaining and most reactionary forces.

The Cuban Family in Transformation

Changes in the family are reflected in the statistics for marriages, divorces, and children. According to studies made by the Cuban Academy of Sciences before 1959, Cuba had a relatively low marital rate, equivalent to less than five unions for every 1,000 inhabitants per year. During the first years immediately after the revolution, the marriage rate rose to among the highest in the world. In 1959-61, Cuban marriage frequency more than doubled the previous rate. Beginning in 1963, the rate leveled off to slightly more than six per year per 1,000 individuals, until 1965, when it again jumped to 8.9 per 1,000 and then returned to the previous figures. In 1968, there was a new rise to more than ten marriages per 1,000 inhabitants, followed by a rise in 1970-71 to thirteen. That rate is not only high in terms of Cuban history, but also is high in comparison with other countries. In 1972 there was a leveling off to nine marriages, which is still quite high. This rate is similar for both rural and urban areas. Divorce statistics for the same period follow similar patterns of net increase.

Housing is a problem which remains one of contemporary Cuba's most difficult areas, even though enormous progress is being made through the microbrigade system. In particular, couples often have to wait several years for their own housing. Alternative solutions include living temporarily, or permanently when the conditions permit, with either the man's or woman's family. There are cases of married couples where the spouses continue to live with their respective families, husband and wife coming together on weekends, for brief beach vacations, or for an occasional night in a hotel. In spite of these serious although transitional inconveniences, neither the marriage rate nor the enthusiasm for having children seems to have been significantly affected.

An analysis of the marital data relates the increases to the fact that free unions were legalized after the revolution, at times in large groups. Furthermore, the general enthusiasm generated by real people's power motivated men and women to establish new families when previously they might not have taken that step. Most important, though, is that the relief from dire necessity and a hope for the future based on real change in the present, such as job security, urban and agrarian reform, health care and education assured for all, enabled people to undertake family commitments and responsibilities.

Religion, which prior to the revolution played a stultifying social role in Cuban family life, has diminished considerably in its social influence, while remaining accessible to all who feel its need. While believers participated in the revolutionary process during the insurrectional period, not a few Catholic and Protestant churches became covers for counterrevolutionary activity. However, as long as churches limited themselves to religious teachings, they were not closed. Freedom of religion has always been a tenet of the Cuban revolution. The government has gone to great lengths to provide religious communities with necessary items (kosher meat, communion wafers, candles, paint for church buildings) even during times of most severe rationing and scarcity.

Relations between the Catholic, Protestant, and Jewish communities, and the revolutionary government have improved as these communities have taken a less separatist position with regard to the revolutionary process. Almost all existing churches have issued declarations in favor of a system "actually carrying out what we have always preached," have come out against the U.S. economic blockade, and have encouraged their membership to take part in voluntary work. The Cuban revolutionary government was among the first to recognize the importance of the widespread progressive Christian movement in Latin America. A number of international meetings of church people have been held in Havana in the seventies. The new socialist constitution proclaims and defends absolute religious freedom, and Cuban laws punish those who, from a position of secular power, would attempt to curtail that freedom or offend or withhold civil rights from believers.

Under Batista's government, the African religions so intimately linked to Cuban culture were prohibited. The *bembés*[7] and other ceremonies took place anyway, of course, with petty officials reaping the benefits of protection money. With the revolution, Cuba legalized the African religions. Although the new generations who receive a scientific education tend to move away from the superstitions and rites of luck, cleansing, and initiation, Yoruba[8] culture, a popular tradition rich in song, dance, poetry, chant, and design, is encouraged in its full dimension. Folklore dance troupes and groups all over the country now depict the old customs, instruments, and attire with the old men and women who traditionally carried this art from one generation to another serving as supervising specialists. In the schools, special instruction is given in the music and dances involved.

A few sects, such as the Jehovah's Witnesses, have been strongholds of reaction and even, at times, of counterrevolution. Not surprisingly, the U.S.-backed Jehovah's Witnesses increased their fieldwork on the island after 1959, especially influencing people in the most culturally backward areas. For more than a decade, the government and party struggled with this problem.

[7] A *bembé* is an African religious ritual.

[8] The Yoruban people flourished in West Africa. Many of the Africans brought to Cuba came from this area.

Pro-revolutionary forces engaged in the long patient task of convincing Jehovah's Witnesses converts that they had made a serious mistake. Converts could lose their lives by adhering to doctrines that refused medical attention and blood transfusions. Jehovah's Witnesses also teach their children not to salute the flag and prohibit them from joining the Pioneer Movement. When dissuasion was not sufficiently effective, the revolution opted to censure this tendency by law.

Although there is no longer any significant tension between the Cuban government and Catholic, Jewish, and Protestant denominations, visits to such churches find their congregations made up almost entirely of older people. Most young people, educated in materialist and scientific principles, no longer feel the need for religion, as their parents and grandparents did. Many find a similar emotional experience in the revolution itself. Building a "kingdom of heaven" on earth, here and now, no matter how complex and difficult the process, is more real and all-involving to most than the vague promise of that "justice after death."

The role of the Cuban mother also has been modified. Although some former traits remain, the present role models are totally different, and in twenty years the changes have been extraordinary. The pre-revolutionary models consisted of the obedient wife, the pure religious woman, the constant protector of her children, and the handservant of her husband: in short, the Spanish model.

Today, the Cuban mother is urged to go out and work. She is encouraged to participate in political and decisionmaking activities. And she receives support, education, and job training, and the moral and emotional stimulus to facilitate what she is doing. The internationalist mother, who might spend months as a construction worker in Vietnam or as a teacher in Angola, is praised and regarded by group love and appreciation. The mothers of the revolutionary martyrs, those who sacrificed their own sons and daughters so that the life Cubans now enjoy might come about, literally acquire hundreds and thousands of sons and daughters with an entire people revering them, caring for them, and holding them up as examples.

The voluntary movement called Militant Mothers for Education (*Madres Combatientes de la Educación*) are housewives organized as school paraprofessionals. Similar movements are organized in other areas of mass work. Housewives are especially active through the local Revolutionary Defense Committees, the Federation of Cuban Women and the National Association of Small Farmers.

Mother's Day in Cuba is practically a national holiday, but it is accompanied by none of the commercialized gift-giving typical of advanced industrialized societies. The Cuban custom involves sending postcards with special messages not only to one's own mother but to mothers one especially wishes to honor. This year, twelve and a half million of these cards were sold. The CDRs cooperate with the postal system to provide voluntary labor, mostly young people, in all neighborhoods so that every card is delivered on Mother's Day.

If Mother's Day is big, International Women's Day is even bigger. On March 8, men in workplaces and on the block get together through the mass organizations to put on parties and cultural activities for women. International Women's Day in Cuba is also a day when the people, in general, turn their attention to women all over the world in recognition of their struggles and achievements.

Racism, a corroding influence from colonial times through the pseudorepublic, has far less impact on the family than it once had. Institutionalized discrimination has disappeared entirely, and individual prejudice, where it exists, has no context in which to flourish. Intermarriage is a natural part of Cuban life. Among the national role models are numerous black men and women such as Antonio Maceo, Lidia Doce, Clodomira Ferrals Acosta, Lázaro Peña, who headed the National CTC until his death in 1974, and Juan Almeida, Commandante of the revolution who heads the party in Oriente province. Today, blacks take their rightful place in all areas of government, the party, and administration. Marta Depréss and Julia Arredondo are black women who were appointed to the Central Committee of the Cuban Communist Party at the 1975 First Congress. Teofilo Stevens, a world amateur boxing champion, is a delegate to the National People's Assembly, and leading dancers in the Cuban National Ballet are black, which was unheard of before the revolution.

Among the most honored of all Cuban women is Mariana Grajales, mother of Antonio Maceo, one of the generals who led the wars of independence in 1868 and 1895. Mariana Grajales went to the front at the age of sixty! Her husband and three of her sons were eventually killed in battle. She had been born in Santiago de Cuba of black Dominican parents, and had thirteen children, among whom was Antonio. She is particularly remembered on Mother's Day.

It hasn't been as easy to overcome traditional family role models as it has been to deal with racism. This is still one of the major obstacles to putting into full practice the changes in the family structure legislated by the government and based on new relationships to production. Sexism in Cuba is rooted in the particular Spanish tradition and is deep and tenacious. Early stories of Cuban leaders who, in the first years of the revolution, made rousing speeches to get women into the labor force and then went home to their own wives whom they wouldn't allow to work are still painful memories. The Family Code which went into effect in 1974 has made great changes, initiating discussions and changes in behavior which are still in progress.

Homophobia, one of the many forms of sexism, is deeply ingrained in Cuban culture. The Declaration of the 1971 Congress on Education and Culture termed homosexuality "a social pathology." There followed a period of heightened discrimination against those who projected their homosexual preference or identity. In the intellectual world, this took the form of frequently not choosing known homosexual writers or performers to represent the country at international events.

It is important to note that the revolutionary government has never passed any discriminatory laws with regard to job placement, education, or housing based on sexual preference. The attitude found in Cuba toward homosexuality predates the revolution, coming from distortions in and among the people. As the seventies drew to a close, attitudes and practices regarding homosexuality became more flexible. In 1979, an entirely new initiative based on a scientific and socially oriented perception began in this area. German experts in the field had been working with Cubans for a number of years, and their efforts included the publication of three books: one aimed at young people, another at adults, and a third at teachers, psychologists, and other specialized personnel. A daily column which answered the most frequent sexual questions asked by youth, including those dealing with homosexuality, began to appear in *Juventud Rebelde*, the afternoon paper.

For the first time in Cuba, this new literature defined homosexuality as a normal sexual choice based on the fact that it includes the characteristics of a healthy relationship between willing adults. Cubans are urged to regard gay men and women as useful and valuable members of society, to be judged as all others are, and most certainly not to be discriminated against or repressed for their sexual preference. This is a major breakthrough in Cuban ideology. Generations may be needed for this assessment to be internalized by the Cuban people, but it is highly significant that the first comprehensive research and its conclusions should put forth such an evaluation.

Mass Organizations

The Revolutionary Defense Committees, the Federation of Cuban Women, the National Association of Small Farmers, the Cuban Workers' Committees, and other mass organizations play an extraordinarily important role in involving family members, irrespective of generational differences, in community and collective endeavors. These are powerful forces in society, and they have a very deep bearing on changing family roles.

Through the CDR, parents, their children, and, in many cases, their grandparents as well, take part in family sports events, where all ages get together to run and do gymnastics and other activities of this type. Women's yearly Pap tests and preventive health care for the whole population are administered by the people through the CDRs in conjunction with the Ministry of Public Health. Community control, recycling of paper and bottles, blood donations, and the cleaning and beautifying of the neighborhoods, are all tasks organized through this mass organization. The CDR keeps records of how the block's young people are doing in school, and acts as coordinator when closer relations between teachers and parents are required. Lay judges for the people's courts are elected by CDR membership, and the new People's Power system also relies on this grouping of three million Cubans in the organization of its grass roots level elections. If the new Cuban family is extended in any way, this extension takes place through the cooperation of the great majority of the block through the CDR.

One of the things that has most affected family relationships during these years of revolution is the fact that all family members spend much less time than before in the home. Many children attend boarding schools where they only come home on weekends. Students from junior high school up, who are not in schools of this type in the countryside, do yearly stints of forty-five days field work away from home. Young and older adults often spend from a week or fifteen days to several months doing agricultural work — as the barriers between manual and intellectual work and the divisions between city and countryside break down. Social and political participation entails frequent meetings, and women and children are as likely to be involved in these as men. It is not unusual for a family to see a mother, a father, or some other adult member off for a year or two on an international mission. When the family comes together and can share experiences, ideas, and affection, it is with a sense that time is at a premium; building a new society is a tough job involving all members of that society. New social relations motivate family relations that are more agile, natural, and spontaneous. Gone are the rigid formalities that weighed down the lives of parents and their offspring under capitalism.

The family, as a social unit, has been the object of analysis and transitional legislation during the 1974 FMC Congress, the First Party Congress (1975), in the new Family Code (discussed throughout 1974 and passed at the beginning of 1975), and the socialist constitution (1976). A clear statement of goals emerged in the thesis on "The Role of the Family in Socialism," discussed at the FMC Congress in 1974:

> ... The socialist system makes relations of equality and mutual aid between men and women possible. The family is based on love and for that reason the relationship between parents and children is also based on confidence and reciprocal friendship. Mutual respect in the family, attention to old people

and dedication to the children's education are principles which socialist morality demands.

The family, like society as a whole, once liberated from capitalism, flourishes under socialism.

We must raise our children as new kinds of people, capable of building communism, and possessing the characteristics of the new society we are creating.

In society first material changes and later changes in consciousness—in political ideas, morality, laws, art, etc.—take place.

Remnants of the past remain, old customs weigh on people's minds, especially on the minds of those who were raised in the heart of the old bourgeois society, and it is difficult for them to throw off their moral concepts, which are no longer applicable. Bourgeois influence from outside the country also tries to penetrate the people's minds, in order to slow our march toward socialism.

Men still exist, in many cases calling themselves revolutionaries, who nonetheless allow the entire weight of domestic duties to fall on their own wives and mothers.

The influence of the old society also persists in those who don't want the women in their families to develop and contribute with their work to the advancement of the revolutionary process and its economy.

The Family Code states: "In socialism the family acquires great importance as the natural cell of social development and the basic nucleus within which a communist education must begin, so that children and young people may develop solid and permanent habits of mutual aid, collectivity, love for the socialist homeland, for study and for work, for social discipline and strength of character."

Conclusions

Under socialism, the family continues to be society's basic cell. In Cuba, an entire people are working toward developing new family relations based on the new relations of production inherent in the socialist phase of economic development. While the theoretical problem has been solved in practice, the transitional stage retains many residual habits and remnants of the bourgeois mentality and morality. The class struggle continues in its ideological form, within the family structure.

As I began with a story, imagined but typical, I would like to close with another: something which happened while I was preparing these essays. I had made an appointment with a well-known Cuban physical anthropologist in order to consult with him about the social and family organization of Cuba's earliest inhabitants. We talked at length in the study of his pleasant home. When he had given me some of his ideas and lent me the books I needed, our conversation turned to other areas, and it wasn't long before this middle-aged man began talking about his only daughter, whom he hadn't seen since she was six years old.

He went on to tell me that he and the child's mother had divorced before the end of the war, and, shortly afterwards, his ex-wife had taken her daughter to the United States. She's a woman herself now, in her early twenties, divorced, working. The professor and his daughter have maintained an affectionate correspondence, and he brought out a photograph album he had just bought for the snapshots she had sent over the years. I looked at the changing face of a strong young Cuban-American woman picking flowers, posing in front of her motorbike, beside a young man who wasn't to be her husband very long, smiling in brilliant Kodacolor.

But I was most moved when this man told me that he had recently received, after eighteen years, the first and only letter from his ex-wife. He went to look for the letter, and he handed it to me to read. In it, a woman spoke, hesitatingly, perhaps somewhat stifled by years of non-communication. She is clearly an educated woman, had recently retired from a teaching post, and has had no real financial problems. But the loneliness, isolation, and social alienation coming through the lines of her letter pierced me like pieces of broken glass.

She told her ex-husband that she imagined he might not have heard that she had remarried, but that her second mate and her daughter hadn't gotten along and the marriage had finally ended, once more, in divorce. The marriage had terminated, however, after this man had driven her daughter from the house —

and now that she was living alone, the girl wasn't interested in returning. Retired, this middle-aged woman lived relatively well, but had "nothing to do with her time." "Distances are great," she wrote, and "your daughter and I hardly see each other anymore."

Outside the window of this man's study, I could hear the noises of a typical Havana street, people sharing the day's news with each other, a loudspeaker blaring music from the corner where the local CDR was involved in preparation for the coming International Youth and Students Festival. Banners were going up. Paper flowers were being strung from house to house. Our conversation had already been interrupted briefly by the arrival of an armload of paper flowers designated for this man's balcony and by a neighbor woman who brought his groceries, which she'd picked up along with her own.

I looked out of the window, and picked up the letter again. What a difference in family life, I thought: community involvement, enthusiasm, collectivity — as opposed to alienation in a dying system. I had come to see this man about family organization among Cuba's primitive peoples, and had found a current family situation totally pertinent to my study.

CHAPTER FIVE

To Create Ourselves: Women in Art

*It's not that we represent the revolution. We are the revolu-
tion. A revolution isn't represented by something: a revolution
is this is what we feel—the human being and all the smallest
details of her life and everything she does to enrich herself.*

Alicia Alonso
Director, National Ballet of Cuba

Along a narrow alley in the neighborhood called Juanelo,
deep in the heart of the old Luyanó section of Havana, the small
wooden houses are painted with butterflies, flowers, and a Cuban
flag. Behind fruit trees that almost obscure one of the homes, an
exceptional woman recreates daily a fanciful world that is inextricably part of a socialist future. She is Antonia Eiríz, one of
Cuba's most important painters; a woman whose monsters
loomed on lonely canvases when she was simply another painter.
Since 1970 Eiríz has been at the center of a people's art movement
which she initiated and encourages: the creation of papier maché
artifacts made by people in her neighborhood. More recently,
the activity has spread to other districts.

It is not uncommon to see the old wooden table, covered with
tear sheets from the ends of newsprint rolls, set up on the small
porch. Neighbors, predominantly women whose lives were limited
to washing, ironing, cleaning, cooking, and children before they
met Antonia, come and take their places around the table. Out

come the old newspapers, more newsprint, some modeling wire, a big can of flour and water paste, and paints which, depending on the current situation, may turn out to be anything from genuine temperas to makeshift pharmaceutical gentian violet and mercurochrome. Hands deftly shape turtles, peacocks, boxes, and trays while sharing opinions about the situation in Iran or the recent wedding down the street.

Eiríz has transformed this neighborhood. Seven or eight women and a couple of men have become dedicated papier maché artists. Children have also taken up the craft by making papier maché masks, and a mask contest at carnival time has become a new annual tradition. The application of the papier maché technique to puppet-making is another neighborhood pastime. Dozens of the dolls are stored in a large box at Antonia's house, waiting to make their appearance at plays written and produced for special occasions by people on this block.

One woman looks up from the piece she's shaping and, without interrupting her work, she says, "We usually work at home, but sometimes we come together here and visit while we work. Ten years ago, I didn't know what papier maché was! Last summer, we all worked hard before the Youth Festival.[1] Why, I made more than 2,000 pieces to be used as gifts for the delegates or to be sold at the craft booths set up for the event. This is my life now."

Another woman's accent betrays her Spanish origin. She first worked in papier maché as a child. "In Spain, we modeled with a special paste made of grated paper," she says, "and in Spanish prisons our patriots made figures out of bread dough." The conversation turns to different techniques used in different places. Antonia talks about her recent trip to Moa, on the extreme tip of the island. The Ministry of Culture is sending her all over the country to teach this magic that animates crumpled old newsprint and gives expression to people's talent.

In the village of Yaya, one of the new peasant communities built by the revolution in the Escambray Mountains in the middle of the island, a young woman named Flora Lauten calls the daily rehearsal for a theater group made up of men and women who

---

[1] The XI World Youth and Student Festival was held in Havana in August 1978. Over 18,000 delegates attended from 145 countries.

live in the village. These are laborers, many of whom had never even seen a theatrical production, much less imagined themselves acting in one, before the revolution. Some, in fact, could barely read or write then. Memorizing complex roles is now part of the everyday experience of these people.

It all began more than ten years ago, with the founding of the Escambray Theater Group, which became an integral part of life in that part of the country. After awhile, it wasn't unusual to witness scenes in which local people couldn't wait for the end of a performance: they simply broke into the middle of a scene, voicing opinions and ideas, relating the theater to their own experience. The Escambray Theater had become a vehicle through which social problems were being identified, faced, and resolved.

Flora Lauten was one of the members of the original troupe. After several years, because of an ill child, she decided to move to La Yaya, a new village for country people who previously had eked out an existence under isolated and difficult conditions. The only "professional" was Flora; the rest of the group were local peasants.

Women in La Yaya wrote and produced a play they called *This Mockingbird Has No Owner*. It dealt with local women whose husbands tried to keep them from going to work and the right these women felt they had to take their places in production. The play was successful not only in La Yaya (successful socially as well as artistically, for that village's percentage of women incorporated into the labor force rose sharply), but everywhere it was performed. The group brought their work to Havana in 1974 when they participated in the National Theater Panorama.

Theatrical activities also sprang up in other peasant communities. The Community Development Group, connected to the Ministry of Construction at the national level, encouraged these efforts, and now there are dozens of peasant theater groups across the country. In all of them, the role of women is outstanding.

Herminia Sánchez, another member of the original Escambray Group, is a playwright and actor with talents for getting people together, encouraging collective enthusiasm, and fostering ideas to take root and grow. She was born near the Havana port area. Her father and brothers were dockworkers, so Herminia knew the hardship and corruption of the docks from earliest childhood. Later, she was to make her name in the world of theater and contribute to the Escambray experience.

With her husband, director Manolo Terrazas, Herminia left the Escambray in 1973 to apply some of what they had learned to an urban proletarian context. Political and mass organizations in the port complex were eager to have them start a theater group there and gave them all the needed support. But getting the port workers themselves to show an interest in theater was more difficult. Herminia once told me it took them an entire year of calling daily rehearsals, and having one person or sometimes no one at all show up, before they could establish the necessary habits of consistency among some thirty port workers, men and women, who had shown initial interest.

On the docks, the Terrazas had to struggle against the workers' tendency to make fun of "theater queers" and against the stark fact that eight hours of longshoring often produced little more than the desire to get home to eat and sleep. Moreover, the dockworkers' generally low educational and cultural levels could not be erased overnight. Slowly, the persistence and energy of a few intensely involved people paid off. Herminia wrote *Amante and Penol*, a play about the life and death of Arecelio Iglesias, a labor leader on the Havana docks who was assassinated in 1948. The piece is not simply a history, but deals with pre-revolutionary problems in the port which socialism has solved or is solving, and with problems resulting from a heritage of desperation and crime.

By 1979, the People's Participatory Theater Group, as the dock group calls itself, had three full-length works in its repertory and had toured all of the island's ports. In the Escambray, the dockworkers participated with dozens of national theater groups and several from other countries to share methods and experiences.

Perhaps one of the most interesting aspects of people's theater was expressed by Gladys, one of the first women to work at the Havana docks and an original member of the port theater group:

It's not just the theater we're producing . . . and we are still amateurs, we've still got a lot to learn . . . it's the change that's come over the docks as a result of this experience. Why, no one here ever used to go to the theater. The most you could expect might be that a few dockworkers would frequent the old vaudeville circuit in Havana. Now, hundreds of workers have been turned on to serious theater as a worthwhile activity. Going to a play has become something they like to do in the evening. First, the dockworkers came out of curiosity to see their fellow workers acting. Now, you'll find dockworkers at any performance in the city . . . Also, because of the particular history and the nature of the docks themselves, sexism is perhaps more of a tradition there than anywhere else. It's very deeply rooted, especially in the men who used to control life on the docks before the revolution, and, consequently, among everyone whose lives they affected. Our dramatic presentations have profoundly shaken the erroneous concepts of sexism held by those involved. Some very extraordinary changes have taken place even in the personal lives of many of our actors and actresses. Gradually, this new way of seeing and feeling things is having an effect upon the people down here in general. . . .

The Cuban stage is a place where many great women have left their mark, not only as fine actors but as directors and in many other capacities. Inevitably, one thinks of Raquel Revuelta. Along with her brother Vicente, she founded Teatro Estudio before the revolution. From the late sixties onward, Revuelta — now in her early fifties and a powerful actor — has directed this group of over 100 performers, which is considered by many to be the finest professional theater company in the country. In their small, newly renovated Hubert de Blanck Theater in the Vedado section of Havana, Teatro Estudio consistently puts on plays by new Cuban authors as well as Brecht, Chekhov, Ibsen, and other modern masters. Raquel Revuelta is familiar to many Americans as the woman in the first part of *Lucía*. Revuelta has acted in a variety of other films, including the forthcoming *Lydia and Clodomira*, which portrays the lives of two peasant women, messengers for Fidel's mountain command, who were caught and tortured to death on a mission to Havana in 1958. She noted the following change of emphasis brought on by the revolution:

Actresses were terrified of growing old before. I don't think this is true anymore. Our actresses now are worried about other things. Before, the actress was like an instrument; she read her lines, she memorized them, and that was all. Now, everyone is interested in *what* they're memorizing.

Other exceptional stage and screen actors are Idalia Anreus (*It's Up To You; A Woman, A Man, A City*), Ana Vina, Herminia Sánchez (of the Escambray and Havana port theater groups), Miriam Lierena (who directs as often as she acts), Asennéh Rodríguez, Berta Martínez (who also directs), Susy Monet, and Alicia Bustamante (a fine comedian). Newcomers include María Eugenia García, who has impressed Cuban theater and film audiences with a series of strong performances. From the older generation, there is Margot de Armas, a character actor now in her sixties who can be as comfortable doing a demanding monologue in a park or factory as she is performing in a formal theatrical setting. Gilda Hernández deserves special note for her work as a writer, actor, and director with the Escambray Theater.

Thelvia Marín comes from a family of artists. She is a poet, writer, and sculptor. It is in this last capacity that she has become best known. An old time communist from the years of pre-revolutionary struggle, Marín began to work in the new government's diplomatic corps soon after the 1959 victory. She was Cuba's cultural attaché in several countries, but she never ceased looking for an opening to take at least a temporary leave from that field to dedicate herself full time to her first loves: ceramics and sculpture in clay, wood, stone, and bronze.

During the 1970s, Marín could be found working in an old semi-abandoned chapel on the grounds of the mental hospital officially called "twenty-seventh of November" but often referred to by its former name, "Quienta de Dependients" or "The Employees' Clinic." Here, two or three highty-trained assistants helped put the finishing touches on the cast for a fifteen-foot-high monument to Serafín Sánchez and Lino Amézaga, heroes of the wars of independence.

Marín was born in the province of Sancti Spíritus, and the two-figured monument is planned for the People's Palace in that provincial capital. Serafín Sánchez was an outstanding figure of the war of 1895, but his home town had to wait for the 1959 revolution for a statue to his memory. Lino Amézaga was a slave who fought under Sánchez in 1868 and again in 1895, rising to the rank of major, and dying before a Spanish firing squad. Amézaga, who was born in what is now Angola and brought to Cuba in slavery, fought for the freedom of his new land. A century later, many of Amézaga's Cuban descendants would travel back to help free his native land from colonialism.

The statue of Sánchez shows him standing, his left hand resting on Amézaga's shoulder. The black man is seated with a book in one hand and a rifle in the other. Amézaga did, in fact, learn to read and write on the battlefield, and Sánchez was his teacher. Townspeople in Sancti Spíritus became so involved in this work-in-progress that a spontaneous collection was taken up, with people contributing bronze household artifacts to be melted down and used in the finished work, the largest ever to be cast in Cuba. In 1979, Thelvia Marín spoke of her work as she climbed the scaffolding:

> We don't yet have artistic foundries here, only industrial ones. Statues and monuments here were always sent out of the country to be cast. But the workers at one of our oldest industrial foundries, in Guanabacoa, are learning right along with us. That's where we're casting the two figures and the whole series of bas relief pieces that complete this monument.

Nersys Felipe still lives in the small town of Gaune, Pinar del Río, Cuba's westernmost province and, before the revolution, one of the poorest and most isolated. She was born in 1935; her formative years were shaped by the struggle for survival common to all but Cuba's upper classes and especially vivid in the memories of those who lived in the countryside. Felipe worked as a teacher, became involved in puppet theater, wrote radio scripts, and produced juvenile shows for the same media before arriving at her true vocation as one of the country's most gifted writers of children's literature.

When Felipe won the 1975 Casa de las Américas literary prize with her *Cuentos de Guane* (*Tales From Gaune*), the book was like a breath of fresh air among the mass of more or less successful attempts in this complex and difficult field. The Cuban Ministry of Culture was doing everything possible to encourage writers to direct their talents toward the creation of a diverse and rich new children's literature, but results had seemed sporadic until then. Felipe carried off the same prize in 1978 with her *Román Elé*, causing critics and readers to speak about a solid talent in this area, and one from whom many more exciting works might be expected. Her stories combine the whimsical dreamworld children love with real history, free of racism, sexism, and other distortions.

Revolutionary Cuban literature includes the works of other writers like Nersys Felipe. Dora Alonso has written with great success for young people and adults alike and Renée Méndez Capote is still writing for children and adults at the age of seventy-eight. Mirta Aguirre is another outstanding intellectual, researcher, professor, and writer, whose poetry and prose are well known. Her exhaustive studies of *Don Quixote* [2] and Sor Juana Inéz de la Cruz [3] have become obligatory texts even outside the country. The younger Rosa Ileana Boudet is an author of powerful prose and an important theater critic. Josefina Toledo is a Martí specialist whose short stories are interesting and unusual.

Until recently, women were in the extreme minority among Cuba's poets. Perhaps only Fina García Marrúz, Mirta Aguirre, Carilda Oliver, or the much younger and very talented Nancy Morejón were widely known. Morejón is a poet whose other work includes exciting translations of French poets, a splendid book about the nickel miners in eastern Cuba, and important studies on Nicolás Guillén. Her own verse has very much concerned itself with the conditions of being a woman and being black in these years of upheaval. Eleana Rivero has written that:

> It is interesting that the period of the 1950s or of the first criticism affected by the revolution do not project the work of a single woman poet. The emergence of women in leadership positions or as prominent intellectuals corresponds to the first years of the revolutionary process, but it isn't until much

[2] Her best known work on this subject is *La Obra Narrativa de Cervantes* (Havana: Instituto Cubano del Libro, 1971).

[3] Sor Juana Inéz de la Cruz, considered by many to be the greatest woman poet in the Spanish language, was born in Mexico in 1648 or 1651 and died of the plague in that country in 1695. She became a nun as the only means of being able to study and write.

later that the publication of works by women poets begins to merit the attention of critics.[4]

Through the active movement of literary workshops organized and stimulated by the Ministry of Culture, a whole new group of women poets, spanning several generations, has emerged: Minerva Salado, Albis Torres, Yolanda Ulloa, Belkis Cusa Malé, Mirta Yáñez, Georgina Herrera, Lina de Feria, Soleida Ríos, Milagros Gonzáles, Reina María Rodriguez, and Marilyn Bobes, among others. Minerva Salado won the prestigious David prize for previously unpublished poets in 1971 and another major poetry prize in 1977, with her very interesting *Tema Sobre Un Paseo* (*Theme on a Walk*). That same year, Georgina Herrera's *Granos de Sol y Luna* (*Grains of Sun and Moon*) won first mention.

Marta Rojas was a sixteen-year-old black woman just starting to work for *Bohemia*, a popular newsmagazine, when Fidel Castro and other survivors stood trial for the July 26, 1953, attack on the Moncada Garrison in Santiago de Cuba. She convinced the editor to let her cover the story. Her description of the trial, very little of which was able to pass censorship at the time it was written, remains the basis for later research of that crucial event because Rojas was one of the few honest journalists to gain access to the courtroom.

Today Rojas is editor of the international page of Cuba's leading newspaper, *Granma*. Her witness to the early days of the twenty-sixth of July Movement has resulted in a valuable body of writing. She was also one of the first reporters to go to the South Vietnamese jungle in the early days of the struggle against American intervention. To her vivid portrayals of that conflict has been added on-the-spot reporting on the resistance to the Pol Pot regime in Kampuchea. While her writing is outstanding, Rojas is far from the lone woman in the Cuban mass media. Dozens of other women are prominent, and some of the country's most important publications have women editors. Although, under a strict definition, journalism might not be thought of as an art by some, the level of work done by women like Marta Rojas is quite distinct from humdrum daily newswriting.

---

[4] "Las Nuevas Poetas Cubanas," *Areito*. Vol. 5, No. 17, 1978. Pp. 31-35.

Internationally, Cuban dance is often equated with one person: Alicia Alonso. This extraordinary woman, now close to sixty and moving between periods of very poor eyesight and almost total blindness, continues to dance the most difficult modern as well as classical repertoire, choreographs, inspires younger dancers, directs Cuba's National Ballet, and travels with it to stages all over the world. Many critics consider her the greatest living ballet dancer. But Alonso's splendor must not obscure the existence of a host of excellent prima ballerinas such as Josefina Méndez, Aurora Bosch, Mirta Pla, Marta García, Loipa Araujo, and María Elena Llorente. Josefina Méndez, like Alonso, choreographs. Some of these women are skilled in the difficult art of teaching ballet. Laura Alonso, one of the company's best known professors, is also recognized for her work in dance therapy with problem children.

The Cuban National Dance Company, which specializes in modern dance, the country's excellent folklore ballet companies, and the fairly new Camaguey Ballet Company have also produced their share of oustanding female artists. A modern dancer who has received world-wide acclaim is Perla Rodríguez.

There are not many women among the established graphic artists in Cuba. Amelia Peldez, who died in 1968, was one of the few Cuban women active in the European and American art scene before the revolution. Since 1959, new possibilities have opened in the visual arts. Interesting work of a younger generation of artists includes the paintings of Isavel Gimeno, the lithographs of Lilian Cuenta, and the drawings of Zaida del Río.

Cuban poster art has acquired a well-deserved world-wide reputation for excellence. Here, too, men have dominated, but, in recent years, there have been oustanding contributions by women. When the nation failed to reach the goal of a ten million ton sugar harvest in 1970, posters were put up everywhere urging "Turn The Setback Into Victory!" The *v* in the word *revés* (setback) rose to the full height of the poster and became the *v* of *victory*. The creator of that poster was Asela Pérez, graphic artist for the Central Committee of the Cuban Communist Party's Department of Revolutionary Orientation. The well-known and colorful image of Che Guevara pulsing in the middle of tonal waves that surge around him to become a map of South America was done by Elena Serrano, a professor at the National Design School. And the poster that won the 1978 Tenth Annual Graphics Contest, a dove of peace in white letters on a bright blue background, specifically designed for the International Youth and Students' Festival, was also from Pérez's drawing board.

Cecilia Guerra, a designer for the Art and Literature Publishing House of the Cuban book industry, is known for her book jackets. She has been responsible for the jackets of the new universal poetry series, one of the best examples of book design in Cuban publishing. Her cover for a collection of Agosthino Neto's poetry was transformed into a popular poster. The design schools are full of young women students, so the coming years should see substantially greater female participation in this field.

Another area almost exlusively male in Cuba is photography, but, once again, women are beginning to be visible. Maria Eugenia Hoyos ("Marucha") and Mayra A. Martínez, for instance, have won a number of prizes in photographic exhibitions. Martínez of the Havana Saíz Brothers Brigade for younger artists, the is the president of the newly inaugurated photography section organization that groups together the younger creative people in different media.

Among the country's popular singers, as many or more women than men share the spotlight. Elena Bourke, the Martí Sisters, Esther Borges, Ella Calvo, Teresita Fernández, Alina Sánchez, Miriam Ramos, Farah María, Beatríz Márquez, and Marta Valdéz all have their own very different and well-defined musical identities. Ella Calvo is a powerful exponent of Cuban black music; Alina Sánchez is an extraordinary lyric soprano. The Martí Sisters are mainstays in the traditional *trova*.[6] Marta Valdéz composes as well as plays and sings. Teresita Fernández is best known for her marvelous musical arrangements of Jose Martí's poetry; she is a popular figure in Havana's Lenin Park on Sundays, where she strums her guitar and sings among the trees behind the lending library in the hollow.

The new song movement, a vibrant continuation of the old *trova*, has so far come forth with only a single well-known female voice, Sarah González, among dozens of male singers. The move-

---

[6] The *trova* is a popular song in free form which often has a romantic theme; it is related to a Chilean form called *tonada*.

ment, however, does include a number of young women, especially if one takes into account all the developing singers across
the country. Nonetheless, no woman has yet to break through
to exhibit the qualities that make a popular talent.

One very special woman in Cuban music is María Cervantes.
Now in her early nineties, she is still an excellent pianist and she
sings regularly. Her songs are from the traditional repertory of
Cuban music, many composed by her father Ignacio Cervantes
and many composed by herself. Today, she must be helped to
the piano, but when her gnarled fingers touch the keys, they come
to life. Her voice isn't what it was for more than half a century,
but it still brings tears to many eyes.

Among classical musicians, two young women pianists, Ni-
noska Fernández Brito and Nancy Casanova, are especially talented. But these are only two of the numerous women performing
in the symphony orchestras, the various string quartets, the Musical Theater, and the opera.

Cuban filmmaking seems to be a totally male domain. Sara
Gomez, a young black director, died suddenly at the age of thirty-
two before she had finished a single feature-length work. Her
De Cierta Manera (*One Way or Another*) was recently completed by a group of her comrades in the industry. The film has
received rave reviews and deals with, among other things, women's
problems in society. There is some discussion as to exactly how
much of this film remains Sara's and how much belongs to those
who took up where she was forced to leave off. Those who knew
Sara say her imprint is unmistakable. In an interview I did with
her in 1970, Sara spoke of her work and sexism as an obstacle
to woman's full participation:

> My work represents a way for me to realize myself in-
> tellectually and socially. I went to work because I felt my voca-
> tion was filmmaking. I can work without abandoning my home,
> but I have to make a double effort that threatens my mental
> health. The revolution must create better conditions, better
> laundry and ironing services, reorganize the distribution of
> foodstuffs, take more into consideration the problem of work-
> ing women, and wage an ideological campaign against the tradi-
> tional sexist mentality of men.

Looking at the many films in what has become an exceptionally interesting and powerful cinematic industry, one discerns a tendecy to ignore or distort women's roles, even in some productions with a historical base. However, there now seems to be a new consciousness around this problem in Cuban filmmakers, almost all of whom are men. A number of recent releases and projects in process evidence an attempt to deal with this problem. While women were most often portrayed in their full dimension in films specifically *about women* (e.g., *Lucía, Manuela, With the Cuban Women*), current personifications of women in a variety of general interest films have depicted greater depth. This is certainly the case with *It's Up To You, One Way or Another*, and *A Woman, A Man, A City. Lydia and Clodomira* and *Portrait of Teresa*, both released in 1979, went even further along these lines.

Two color documentaries by Marisol Trujillo, the first woman director to surface since Gomez' death, premiered in 1979. *El Lugar En Que Tan Bien Se Esta (The Place You Feel So Good In)*, a short on the city of Havana, and *Lactancia (Nursing)*, young Trujillo's first films, received positive reviews. While women in film have yet to be incorporated in a major way at the highest level, there are numerous women in the industry in key positions. In fact, Cuban cutting rooms are largely run by women at this point. Miriam Talavera, Gladys Cambre, Caita Villalón, Gloria Argüelles, Julia Yip, and Mirita Lores immediately come to mind. In the October 1978 issue of *Revolucion Y Cultura (Revolution and Culture*, the Cuban Ministry of Culture's monthly art magazine), Angel Rivero did an interesting collective interview with these editors. Julia Yip spoke of how she came to the cutting room, "At the present time I'm the editor for the ICAIC [6] Latin American Newsreel, but I began as a secretary. Later I became an assistant editor, and that was the first time I had direct contact with film. From then on, film really began to interest me. Still later I was promoted to editor."

Caita Villalón, who has edited some of Cuba's most impressive pictures (*For The First Time, The First Battle, About a Character Some Call San Lázaro and Others Babalú Ayé*), said:

Montage is one of the aspects of filmmaking that gives us

[6] Cuban Film Institute.

good experience for going on to other specialties. There are
quite a few famous directors who were editors first. It's not
surprising because an editor is in touch with the total process
of any given film. In the cutting room you can save or sink a
picture. . . . Editing is kind of miraculous: you cut a frame
and you can see the film come to life. That's my greatest
satisfaction.

Some of Cuba's most important cultural institutions are directed by women who have helped to forge and carry out a new
people's cultural policy over the past twenty years. Haydée Santamaría, heroine of the Moncada attack, member of the Central
Committee of the Cuban Communist Party and the Council of
State, has headed the Casa de las Américas since its inception
in 1959. The Casa has done more, perhaps, than any other single
institution to break the cultural blockade thrown up to complement the economic blockade against the Cuban revolution.
Through the Casa collective, whose members are predominantly
women, Cuban culture (literature, art, music, theater, etc.) is
promoted throughout Latin America and Latin American works
are presented in Cuba. Santamaría has been an exceptionally vi-
sionary force in the Casa and in Cuban arts.

Alicia Alonso, cited earlier, adds to her work as a great
dancer and fine choreographer by directing the complex activities
of Cuba's National Ballet. Before the revolution, it was the Alicia
Alonso Ballet Company, a private organization whose founder
and director adamantly refused to allow her talent to be used
for Batista's official events. Alonso was concerned with the problems of enabling Cuban ballet dancers to develop their art in a
hostile environment filled with race and class privilege. Since
1959, Alonso has devoted her life, above and beyond her own
personal career as a dancer, to the development of a system in
which future dancers from every segment of Cuban society may
have their training and future employment insured.

Havana's Bellas Artes Museum (The National Art Museum)
is headed by Marta Arjona. She inherited a totally ruling class
pre-revolutionary institution and has slowly turned it into a museum reflecting the true history of Cuban art, enhanced by international exhibitions of every sort. Another key leader of Cuban

cultural institutions is Marcia Leiseca, who directs the Theater and Dance division of the Ministry of Culture.

In a country only twenty years removed from and still suffering the sexist distortions of a colonial and pseudorepublican past, it is clearly even more difficult for women than for men to make unique cultural contributions. Women must catch up with their brothers in terms of a solid educational foundation. Basically, this has been accomplished in Cuba, where as many females as males now study the most varied and specialized arts and sciences. Women are not only emerging as artistic talents in the cities. All Cuban cultural institutions from the Ministry on down — specialized art schools, performing companies, publishing houses, writers workshops, musical groups — are set up to facilitate the promotion of culture in the most remote areas. Bookstores, libraries, mobile film units, traveling theater groups, and concert tours encourage the arts in all parts of the nation.

As with any of the contemporary cultural areas, the developing form and content of Cuban dramatic and cinematic arts is inextricably related to political, social, and feminist consciousness. What is so important about the cultural changes in Cuba is that grass roots people's productions have a place alongside internationally known performers and technically sophisticated film. The Ministry of Culture has understood that while one hand must send local professional talent to Europe, the other hand needs to send theatrical groups and cinema into the countryside. It is through those who have never before had the opportunity to learn, experience, and make, that the revolution seeks to raise an entire people's cultural level, and central to the process is a full role for women.

The Federation of Cuban Women: The Role of a Woman's Organization in the Revolutionary Process

"I tell the women sometimes: our organization is the Federation. Oh, we can even have the honor of belonging to the party, of being a great personage, even a lieutenant or a captain or even a commander! But our own organization is the FMC! We can belong to all the organizations but you've got to understand that this is all ours!"

Haydée Méndez, peasant woman and founder of the FMC in Buey Arriba, Sierra Mountains, in a conversation with the author, summer of 1970.

There has been a great deal of interest in the role of a woman's organization within the revolutionary process. The term "revolutionary process" includes any progressive or revolutionary effort which occurs during a repressive or pre-revolutionary capitalist period, in an insurrectional period, or in a period in which socialist construction is begun. Within the women's movement in the capitalist countries, there are a variety of ideas concerning this question. Radical feminists of different ideological persuasions sometimes opt for separatist organizations with goals not necessarily socialist and perhaps not even reflecting an economic system involving justice for all human beings. On the other hand, many of the more traditional leftist political parties

123

have failed to address themselves in any meaningful way to the very specific problems women have inherited through different historical phases.

The Federation of Cuban Women can be used as a model to clarify the Leninist concept of the need for a semi-autonomous woman's organization under the leadership of a central party. Through the FMC, the importance of such an organization both for the development of the struggle and for women's personal and collective liberation can be demonstrated. Finally, the FMC exemplifies the ways in which this kind of an organization is vital to women's full participation in the process of change, as well as depicting a means enabling the process of change to draw on the resources of all its potential protagonists.

Throughout Cuban history, women have always fought for social progress. There are stirring examples of audacious and patriotic women whose decisive contributions symbolize the attitudes and actions of masses of women at any historic moment. Women were actively involved against the earliest Spanish colonization, the anguish of slavery, the battered pseudorepublic, as they were equally a part of the heroic struggle against Machado and the definitive insurrection which put an end to Batista and U.S. imperialist domination.

But just as the change in 1959 was different from the frustrated partial changes at each step leading to it, so the demands on the Cuban people were different demands. When the people themselves take power, the possibilities on one hand and the obstacles and risks on the other are infinitely greater and more complex. The quantitative aspect of change now becomes qualitative as well. The chains have been snapped. Exploitation and oppression have reached their high points; a collective energy is unleashed, determined never again to suffer that exploitation and oppression. How can this energy be organized so that the people's determination may materialize into a solidly based future?

In Cuba, before 1959, women shared the oppression of the entire working class, with the situation being worse for black women. There were very few women professionals, and women in the countryside were particularly limited educationally, culturally, and economically. Throughout the nation, only nine percent of all women worked outside the home. Most of these were domestic servants who lived and worked in the homes of the wealthy, earning a pittance wage of between $8.00 and $25.00 a month, with almost unlimited hours of work and no job security whatsoever. There were some 100,000 women forced into prostitution by the economic hardships of a system which made Havana a playground for the international elite and a special domain of the Mafia and other criminal elements. Cuba was little more than an American colony, and, within that colony, women were at a disadvantage in their respective class situations.

Once victory came, one of the immediate questions was how to organize Cuban women. There were already a few groups, some of a social nature, others relating to different political movements. In the first few months of 1959, a few more sprang up to support the first revolutionary measures or to speak out for women's rights. The need apparent to all was to unify these groups into a single organization whose objectives would be to strengthen and advance the revolution while at the same time making women conscious of the important role they were to play in the nation's new path, a role that would be on an equal footing with men.

In response to these needs the Federation of Cuban Women was born on August 23, 1960. It opened its ranks to all women, irrespective of class, race, or creed. Recalling those days, Vilma Espín has said:

> Back in 1959, when they talked to us about creating a woman's political organization, we were far from ideologically prepared for that task. Why do I say this? Because I remember we said: What? If we're going to start a woman's organization, does that mean we're going to start an organization of Negroes as well? Are we going to have a different organization here for everyone who suffered a specific kind of discrimination? And I say we weren't ideologically prepared to deal with the task because that was our immediate reaction. As soon as the project got off the ground, the need for such an organization became clear to us. . . .[1]

At that time, the Cuban Revolution had not yet been officially declared socialist. This would not happen until the eve of the invasion of the Bay of Pigs in April 1961. Cultural and ideologi-

[1] Author's interview, 1972.

cal penetration had been such in Cuba that the mere mention of
the words "socialism" or "communism" struck terror into the
imagination of most Cubans. Thus, the FMC began to work at
a time when it was difficult to use Marxist terminology and, in
some cases, even to speak against imperialism. Here was a country,
like so many underdeveloped dependent countries, where to
speak against the cause of the problem was difficult even in the
midst of revolution.

In the face of these difficulties, the FMC boldly set out to
tackle the most urgent problems. The first major efforts included
schools for peasant women. Through them, tens of thousands
of previously isolated women were able to study and eventually
to work. Many early cadres in the rural areas were graduates of
these schools and returned to their villages to share what they
had learned. There were also classes in first aid which were, at
the same time, the seeds of the first women's militia. Concurrently,
the FMC lent a hand in the rehabilitations plans for prostitutes,
which involved complex plans for learning trades and professions
while regaining the most important thing a human being posses-
ses, dignity. With these and other initiatives, the FMC won its
place as the organization women turned to for orientation in
times of crisis and the place where they could offer their ideas
and services to the revolution.

Chile provides a more recent and tragic example of how the
enemy attempts to use women to protect not their interests but
its own, and why a strong and unified organization of revolutionary women becomes a necessity in any process of social change.
A newspaper article in the *Los Angeles Times* (January 31, 1974)
describes the breadth and scope of the counterrevolutionary
women's movement that helped set the stage for the bloody coup
of September 11, 1973. The article is titled "Chile's Women —
Power Behind Allende's Fall," and says, in part:

> Four months after the overthrow of Chile's President
> Salvador Allende, the story is coming to light how clandes-
> tinely organized women's groups played a decisive role in the
> events that led to his downfall. . . .
>
> "Make no mistake, we organized for the express purpose
> of helping to overthrow Allende," declared Maria Armanet

Izquierdo, speaking to a reporter recently. Mrs. Armanet was a member of the executive commitee of a group called *Poder Femenino*. . . .

"If it hadn't been for *Poder Femenino* and its femi-allies, the *Unidad Popular* would probably still be in power today, pushing Chile towards Marxism-Leninism," said Maria Eugenia Oyarzun, a journalist. . . .

The overt manifestations of women's resistance to Allende are well known to the Chilean public: a series of marches and demonstrations that began with the now legendary March of the Empty Pots, in December, 1971 . . . but little is known of the much more important behind-the-scenes feminine activism, particularly the . . . luncheon at which the largest single women's resistance group was born. The organization took the official name SOL, Civic and Family Movement. SOL stands for "solidarity, order, liberty" and the acronym means "sun" in Spanish.

SOL grew into a cadre of more than 40,000 women activists. Each activist held the responsibility of enlisting the aid, when needed, of five other women—a formidable "army" in a nation of 9.26 million.

Although still in its infancy at the time, SOL took part in the March of the Empty Pots, a parade of thousands of middle-class women through this capital's streets. . . .

SOL extended roots into every facet of Chilean national life. These included neighborhood centers, mother's centers, parent-teacher exchanges, hospitals, clinics, private and public offices. A SOL section existed for gathering intelligence and another for covert operations. . . .

Marxism is much more serious for a woman than a man because it's the negation of the family—it separates children from their parents. . . .

It is well-known that great masses of women supported the popular government of Chile, that many women were among the tens of thousands of the coup's victims, and that women are now a fundamental part of the resistance struggle. But this article shows that the opponents of socialism are acutely aware of the importance of organizing women. Unfortunately, the role women are forced to play in capitalism makes them prey to the most reactionary kinds of motivation, such as the call to protect the bourgeois "home," private property values, and religious fanaticism. Secondly, the article also illustrates the class nature of counterrevolution. "Thousands of middle-class women" marching with empty pots is an unwitting exposé of the contradiction inherent in women whose stomachs have been feigning hunger while hundreds of thousands of their working class sisters and brothers are for the first time involved in the conquest of the kind of freedom which feeds everyone! "If it hand't been for *Poder Femenino* and its femi-allies, the *Unidad Popular* would probably still be in power today..." confirms the fact that the UP was, in fact, a government democratically elected by the majority of the people.

When the article defines Marxism as the "negation of the family," it is using one of its oldest manipulative devices to distort reality. In Cuba, rumors spread like wildfire that "the government's going to tear your children from your arms and send them off to Russia...!" It is ironic that imperialism, the system which actually does take young people from their families and sends them off to kill and be killed around the world (or kills them off at home with drugs and alienation), tries to instill this fear in people engaged in a process in which, for the first time, parents can see their children grow up well-fed, clothed, healthy, educated, and in control of their own future!

Cuban women today, who were among those who first united in the common effort of defending their hard-won revolution back in 1959, reminisce about the early days of that defense. In Cuba, too, there were "empty pot marches," although they hardly managed to attract more than a couple of hundred pathetic middle-class women. One of today's Federation leaders recalls those early days:

> ...One day we heard that the counterrevolution was organizing a group of women to march in a certain section of the city. We all piled into a couple of old cars we had then and in no time we were right on the spot where those women had gathered! There was no need of police or army; we just formed a compact body right in front of those women and we began to demonstrate *for* our revolution.... The moral aspect

of our presence alone caused them to disband and disperse before their march ever got under way. . . . We started climbing back into the cars we'd come in, and it was then that I remember how amazed we all were that so many of us had been able to fit into those few vehicles!!![2]

In 1959 and 1960, the counterrevolution was everywhere: instilling fear in people through constant unfounded rumors, hoarding necessity items and disrupting distribution, draining the nation of skilled technicians, doctors, and other needed professional people. The United States, while ghettoizing Puerto Ricans and Mexican migrant workers, opened its arms to Cuban exiles "fleeing communism," from the small dependent bourgeoisie down to the drug-dealers, pimps, and other criminals. This was part of the plan whose major tools were economic blockade, diplomatic pressure on other countries, and direct military intervention.

In the Cuban revolution's first years, some of the bourgeoisie and most of the middle class stayed on, hoping to be able to help provoke the downfall of the people's government. Bourgeois and middle class women, those who in Chile founded *Poder Femenino*, certainly had their potential Cuban counterparts. 70,000 maids worked in the homes of these women. One of the first strong manifestations of class conflict as a result of the Cuban revolutionary victory was these women's struggle for the right to attend the schools set up by the revolutionary government so they could begin to change their lives.

The newly-founded Federation was central in running these schools for domestic servants. Along with reading and writing, basic math, dressmaking, and a variety of skills designed to channel them into more rewarding areas of work, these women took courses called "Revolutionary Instruction." What precisely was this "Revolutionary Instruction"? It wasn't theory. It wasn't abstract. It wasn't called Marxism-Leninism. It was a simple and clear explanation of what the revolution saw as its goals, what its problems were, why and how the people have a right to the land they work and the homes they live in, why everyone must have

---

[2] From a conversation in 1971 between the author and Carolina Aguilar, director of the magazine, *Mujeres*, and a member of the National Executive Board of the FMC.

the right to free medical attention, education, work, food, and relaxation. It addressed the interests the enemies of the revolution protected through their campaigns. These courses armed the women ideologically so they would be better equipped to face the rumors launched and perpetrated by their "mistresses." Through the courses, some of the most marginal and exploited Cuban women learned where their real class interests lay. Avoided were scenes such as those common in Chile during the last year of the Popular Unity government, where maids stood in lines and echoed ruling class complaints about shortages or engaged in speculation.

The Cuban women who fought in the mountains and the cities, who had been engaged in every level of struggle during the insurrection, were women of vastly differing social origins, ideological persuasions, educational levels, geographical situations, and mobilization capacities. Some were among the revolutionary leadership, conscious of the role they would be called upon to play in the new society. But great masses of women revolutionaries understood only in the most instinctive way "that Fidel and his army of rebels were fighting for a better life for them all. . . ."

In Cuba, the first women to unite and found the Federation of Cuban Women came from the Twenty-sixth of July Movement, the Student Directorate, the old Communist Party (PSP), and the labor movement. They also came from literary societies, social clubs, groups of Catholic dames, and independent women who simply were able to see and understand the need for organized action.

At the founding meeting, on August 23, 1960, Fidel spoke of Cuban women's tradition of heroism and responsibility, and he summarized the national situation at that moment: a revolution already being attacked economically, militarily, and culturally by the enemy to the north. The U.S. blockade had been put into effect, sabotage was rampant from outside the country as well as from within. A nation that had been forced to produce and consume for centuries according to the needs of foreign exploiters was suddenly on its own and having to share the time and effort devoted to construction with the time and effort devoted to defense.

The immediate tasks were those that had to be tackled in the initial follow-up to victory. This work involved building, organizing, equipping, and staffing the first day care centers, responding to armed aggression and invasion with first aid brigades, militia, and substituting in the factories to maintain production levels; organizing a school program for domestic servants and peasant women; contributing thousands of Federation members to work in the year-long literacy campaign; providing the first teachers in the rural areas. In short, women shouldered the gun, the notebook, the machete, and the medical kit, and pitched in to help defend and consolidate the revolution.

Vilma Espín has said that when comrades ask her how women were first brought together, she tells them that one of the first attractions were the classes in first aid and dressmaking. Women were interested in acquiring those skills. At the same time, the first sabotage was taking place and some enemy planes had already been in action. Thus, the process of teaching the masses that the real name of the enemy was imperialism went hand in hand with the improvement of daily life. The revolution had not yet called itself socialist, but women, in organized classes, were already speaking about the role they wanted to play in the newly emerging society.

At the FMC's First Congress, in 1962, these concepts and objectives had become absolutely clear not only to the revolution's vanguard leadership, but to its masses who were in the process of organization. Concrete reality, practice, and theory was the dialectic that pushed this movement forward in all sectors of Cuban society. The organization and heightening of mass social and political consciousness was parallel and related among men, women, youth, in the Revolutionary Armed Forces, among the workers, peasants, and those who had fought and won the war and those who only afterwards saw the justice of the struggle and decided to become a part of it. Each sector moved forward at its own pace, commensurate with class and other factors. The organization's program and statutes were set forth and passed on by the delegates. The introduction to the original statutes began thusly:

The Federation of Cuban Women, founded in 1960 with

the goal of uniting all our women and incorporating them into
the process of change which began with the revolutionary victory of January 1959, and having developed, grown and
strengthened itself extraordinarily within that process of change,
now finds itself before a new and important goal: that of
enabling Cuban women to efficiently and fully take their places
in all phases of socialist construction.[3]

Until 1962, the FMC did not consider a massive incorporation of women into production as one of its goals. Such an
orientation wasn't even set forth in the long range economic planning of the time. But as the revolutionary process unfolded, it
became clear that women's participation in social production
was essential to development. The FMC began to train women
to occupy all vacancies in the labor force as a priority task. Grass
roots activists became very clear about the need to incorporate
women into production and to train women for job categories
that they had never before contemplated filling.

This required complex coordination and competence at
many different levels. Special training programs were instituted
to provide women with the skill needed to take a role in production. Courses were designed for housewives, enabling them
to acquire expertise without having to abandon transitional
domestic tasks. Eventually, the new Family Code and other
legislation urged men to carry their full share of the responsibility for housework and child care. At the same time, the initial
literacy campaign was followed up by a national drive to provide
at least a sixth grade education for the entire adult population.
By 1980, masses of women were being educated in regular as
well as specially designed courses at universities and technical
institutes. The list of skilled specializations available in the
sciences, medicine, engineering, economics, and all other subjects
was as long and as detailed as for men. The statistical breakdown
of the process is staggering. In 1976-77, there were 260,694 wom-
en enrolled in adult education. This represented 37.2 percent of
all adults. In the previous year, as part of the drive to have all
adults achieve a sixth grade diploma, 120,947 women had been
involved.

The FMC has evolved channels to bring community initia-

---

[3] From a mimeographed pamphlet on the Statutes distributed within the FMC.

tive quickly to the attention of those in decisionmaking positions, and vice-versa. Federation leadership was instrumental in raising consciousness, in 1974, about the low percentage of women in party and administration leadership and the insufficient number of women delegates in the initial People's Power project in Matanzas. The organization's Second National Congress, in November of 1974, studied many of the more complex superstructural problems still facing women, and came up with recommendations which were treated in even more depth at the First Communist Party Congress held the following year.

The Federation was active in all areas where women faced problems or had talents to contribute to society. Many of these areas have become special fronts or commissions within the organization: production, ideology, education, voluntary work, social work, day care, coordination between women and the army, and women and the peasant movement.

As of 1980, the FMC had a membership of 2,312,472 members, which is eighty-one percent of all the women in Cuba over age fourteen. Of this more than two million membership, fifty-eight percent are housewives. There were 50,557 *delegacions* (the grass roots block level) and 9,992 *bloques* (larger geographical areas). In all of these units, there was massive participation. The FMC was sponsoring over 2,000 gymnastic groups involving 54,452 women, while 73,623 women were active in agricultural brigades in the countryside. There were 47,892 history activists at the *delegación* level and 9,644 at the *bloque* level who dealt with community, personal, family, and organizational history. Over 100,000 women were involved in friendship brigades which worked with women from other countries. Almost 200,000 women were active in agitational and propaganda groups while some 60,000 worked in public health brigades. A million and a quarter women were involved in the 14,892 Militant Mothers for Education Brigades. The FMC also ran nearly 2,000 dressmaking schools with an enrollment of 38,243. Another 31,052 women already had graduated from such schools. The monthly magazine *Mujeres* (*Women*) dealt with all areas of interest to women, providing material for personal study or for analysis at the monthly base level meetings.

The fundamental objectives of the FMC could be summed up in six major points:

1. To raise the self-esteem and image of women in society.

2. To make women conscious of the value and necessity of their participation in all facets of society.

3. To raise women's ideological, political, and cultural level in order that women be in the best possible position to play the role women must in the construction of socialist society.

4. To channel, from the grass roots upwards, women's opinions, ideas, and problems in order that they may be presented to the party and state agencies for solutions. In some cases these solutions will be material, in others they will be legal, in still others, political or ideological.

5. To offer the revolution the energies and ideas of the fifty percent of the population which is female.

6. To share experiences with sister nations and to demonstrate that only through socialist revolution may a just society be attained, a classless society in which women are truly free.

For Cuba, the dynamics of mass consciousness-raising has been a balanced process involving both form and content. Each task has prepared women ideologically for the tasks to come while, at the same time, creating the objective conditions making possible those next steps. In this way, the residual incapacitating prejudices are being replaced by a real understanding of women's cultural, social, political, and economic needs and roles. As the nation moves forward, those needs and roles increasingly become one and the same. Economic independence and, as a result, equality in all spheres, is the absolute prerequisite for women's liberation. The FMC began by addressing itself to the inequalities wrought by centuries of discrimination, gradually becoming the launching pad for raising consciousness about the more subtle residual inequalities. As some problems and differences have disappeared, one area after another has ceased to come under the auspices of a specifically woman's organization. An example of this is the militia. At first, there was a militia for women within the Federation, but once women became accustomed to engaging in the military defense of their country, the "women's" militia ceased to exist; women simply joined the national militia which was now for men and women.

While the Cuban revolution proceeds, as always, in its own unique style, its leadership has been deeply influenced by what Lenin wrote when discussing the problem of organizing women with Clara Zetkin in 1920:

> ... we need to work systematically with our masses of women. We must call on those women we have been able to help out of their once passive position, we must draft them and arm them for the working class struggle. . . . I'm not only talking about proletarian women who work in the factories or slave in their homes, but about the peasant women as well, about women from different sectors of the petit-bourgeoisie. They too are victims of capitalism. . . . They too are prey to an apolitical psychology, an unsocialized backward mass of women with narrow and limited horizons. It would be inconceivable, completely inconceivable not to pay attention to this situation. We need to develop our own special methods of agitation and organization. We're not talking about a bourgeois defense of "women's rights," but about the practical interests of the Revolution.[4]

In the period of socialist reconstruction, which has gone on in Cuba for twenty years and is still in process, for structural as well as for superstructural reasons, women continue to have to catch up with men in terms of social and economic roles. Consciousness-raising has been and will continue to be accompanied by the strengthening of the economic base as all means — educational, legal, organizational — are used to further a dialectical understanding and resolution of the remaining problems. Women's gains in Cuba are still in the transitional phase; but the direction of national policy is clear. The FMC has been crucial in leading the struggle and will continue to be crucial in the struggles which lie ahead.

[4] *Lenin on the Emancipation of Women* (Moscow: Progress Publishers, 1968).

Appendixes

III. OBJECTIVE AND SUBJECTIVE ELEMENTS WHICH PREVENT FULL PARTICIPATION OF WOMEN. ANALYSIS OF THE PRESENT PROBLEMS OF WORKING WOMEN

The socialist revolution has established the bases that guarantee the rights of women, giving them full equality with men. But, do women really exercise all these rights? What factors prevent them from doing so?

Situations of inequality (thoroughly examined in the Second Congress of the FMC) persist. Such situations exist not solely as a consequence of material difficulties, which will be eradicated in the process of economic development, but also because criteria and attitudes contrary to the postulates and laws of our socialist society are frequently maintained.

A fundamental battle must be waged in the sphere of consciousness, where backward, antiquated concepts still persist.

Discrimination against women has existed for many centuries. It dates from the disintegration of the primitive community and the concomitant establishment of private property and division of society into classes; at that time, men gained both economic supremacy and social predominance.

Throughout the various periods founded on the exploitation

[1] *Sobre El Pleno Ejercicio de la Igualdad de la Mujer: Tesis y Resolution,* Editado por el Departamento de Orientación Revolucionaria del Comité Central del Partido Comunista de Cuba, La Habana, 1976. Translated by Dennis and Joan M. West.

of man by man, women either remained relegated to the home, with limited participation in social production, or else they were unduly exploited.

These concepts, which prevailed in our country until the overthrow of the capitalist system, can have no place in the constructive stage of the new society.

As integral members of the permanent labor force, as well as in innumerable voluntary tasks over the years, women have unquestionably demonstrated a sense of responsibility, intellectual capabilities, leadership potential, stability, decisiveness, and dynamism.

Hundreds of thousands of *compañeras* [2] have overcome real difficulties in order to fully participate in revolutionary tasks and in order to contribute to the construction of socialism.

They have participated in the creative endeavors of education and culture.

They have demonstrated that they are capable of leading, of developing economic plans, and of carrying out the work of the party.

They have shared the same trenches in the face of enemy aggression, ready to give their lives for the revolution.

The Cuban woman has demonstrated thoroughly that she is capable of accomplishing whatever jobs she is assigned.

Consequently, the party, state agencies, enterprises, and political and mass organizations must beware of unjust criteria and decisions which oppose the revolution's goal of eliminating women's inequality.

To this end, and in order to provide a just solution to each case, the following recurring situations, which presently limit women's complete integration into social activity, must be taken into account:

— When men are given preference for available positions on the pretext that "women have a lot of problems."

---

[2] In this document a *compañera* denotes the revolutionary or new woman. *Compañera* (f.) — or *compañero* (m.) — in contemporary Cuban usage means "friend" or "comrade." It is used now both among political people and those who are simply friendly. At the beginning of the revolution, it was used almost exclusively as the common form of address. Preceded by *mi* (my), it usually means "my husband" or "my wife" in the sense of a committed relationship which may or may not be legitimated by marriage.

— When, in the process of determining political or administrative promotion, this right is denied women in order to avoid possible difficulties occasioned by the demands of home and family.

— When an exemplary *compañera* is judged harshly because of a tardy entry into the militia or for not having participated in permanent mobilizations, volunteer labor, or study — without bearing in mind that she alone cared for the children, the sick, or the elderly of her family.

— When esteemed *compañeras* are unjustly criticized on the basis of false criteria concerning so-called "moral problems."

Housework: Women's Unjust Overload of Work

The first three situations exemplify the inequality which establishes an unfair situation for women. We are referring to the extra effort that the working woman expends when she alone does the housework after having finished her working day; this limits her participation and implies a greater expenditure of energy on her part.

If we add up the amount of time that she spends going from home to workplace, taking the children to a day care center or school, shopping for foodstuffs and manufactured products, washing and ironing, cooking, cleaning, caring for the children and the family's sick and elderly, we can see clearly that the working woman will have to make a great effort to study and that she will dispose of very little or no time to participate in recreational or cultural activities or to rest. Add to this, oftentimes, the time devoted to activities of mass and political organizations.

The situation of the woman in those homes where the entire family shares the housework is completely different. Such a situation establishes a relationship of complete equality and comradeship, and contributes to the success of the marriage and to the education of the children in the just principles of the revolution.

A survey of 251 working women taken in April of this year revealed that, on the average, they expend thirteen hours a day Monday through Friday working at the workplace and at home, and eleven and a half hours a day on weekends, owing to the accumulation of housework.

Women's Integration into the Labor Force and Job Tenure

In order to conquer underdevelopment, society needs the contributions of all its members, both men and women.

The creation of the necessary material conditions which depend on economic development will be reached more rapidly to the extent that a greater number of women contribute to the productive process.

In order to evaluate the efforts expended in reaching a sum total of more than 600,000 working women, the following chart is presented to illustrate the result of the integration of women into the work force and their job tenure during the period 1969-1974:

Year	Women Integrated	Net Increase	Decrease
1969	106,258	25,477	
1970	124,504	55,310	
1971	86,188	—	63,174 *
1972	130,843	37,263	
1973	138,437	72,279	
1974	127,694	69,748	
	713,924	196,903	

As these statistics show, the positive fact of integration is accompanied by a negative one: pressured by objective and subjective difficulties confronting them in the family and social milieu, a large number of women, including professionals and technicians, remove themselves from productive activity.

* This figure does not correspond exactly to 1971 because it includes dropouts that date back to 1967. In 1971, there was an updating of the records for all women who had dropped out of the work force; during this process, many administrators informed the National Bank of Cuba of definitive drop-outs not previously reported.

In order to achieve an increment of 196,903 working women in the 1969-1974 period, it has been necessary to incorporate 713,924 women.

No revolutionary should be indifferent to the serious situation caused by a woman leaving her employment, since this obstructs economic goals and harms the development of a revolutionary consciousness in women and in the people in general.

Rights and Duties of Working Women

The working woman's full enjoyment of her rights implies the fulfillment of creditable duties. Women should understand this reality and realize that the difficulties confronting them will be partially alleviated as the state is able to allocate resources for the expansion of institutions and services which will solve many of the problems of the working family.

These resources will be the result of increased production and productivity, which will be accomplished through everyone's efforts.

Men and women in this new society have the duty of working conscientiously, maintaining labor discipline, meeting standards and finishing jobs, raising productivity, increasing the quality of production, caring for and strengthening socialist property, and enthusiastically participating in socialist emulation[3] in order to stimulate production and improve the quality of services.

Some Material Solutions to the Problems of Working Families

The revolution has made great efforts to alleviate housework and to guarantee the best child care by creating appropriate institutions and implementing services.

Day care centers, boarding schools, scholarships, workers' dining halls, priority systems for working women via the CTC-

[3] *Socialist emulation* is a process of competition in which individuals within a group mutually assist each other toward the achievement of collectively agreed upon group goals. *Socialist emulation* encourages a spirit of intra- and inter-group cooperation, quite different from the cut-throat, dog-eat-dog capitalist approach to competitive activities.

MINCIN card,[4] pre-sale plans in grocery stores, and special considerations in dry cleaning establishments and laundries have all contributed to fulfilling this objective.

654 day care centers, enrolling approximately 55,000 children in the 1974-1975 school year, benefit 47,926 families.

Boarding schools enroll 220,800 students. MINED scholarships[5] and "Camilo Cienfuegos" military schools account for 298,000 students, without considering those receiving scholarships from other agencies.

Vacation plans, camps, and special areas for children of working mothers are presently being developed for the Pioneers.

Plans for the next five years call for the construction of 400 day care centers (which will increase the enrollment to some 150,000 children), several hundred boarding schools, and scores of special schools and homes for the elderly and for invalids.

The scholarship system will be capable of benefiting about 700,000 students in 1980.

Given the material resources of the country and the many other necessities which must be satisfied, it is not possible at present to achieve much more in this area. These figures represent great efforts and, although we know that they do not meet our needs, they do constitute the maximum possibilities for the 1976-1980 period.

In addition to increasing the number of educational institutions for children, we have, in recent years, achieved a better usage of available services and the expansion of previously existing ones.

Also, sales of refrigerators, stoves, washing machines, blenders, sewing machines, and other electrical household appliances have increased.

The solutions, which have required great resources and ef-

---

[4] The *CTC-MINCIN* card is a worker's union membership card issued by the Cuban Trade Union in conjunction with the Ministry of Domestic Commerce (*Ministerio de Comercio Interior*). The priority system for working women allows them to shop on the first day of their group's buying period, thus enabling women who work to avoid long lines and to have a wider selection of consumer items. Before this system was instituted, workers were inadvertantly penalized by the best goods being purchased by non-working persons who could afford to wait hours in lines.

[5] Scholarships given by the Ministry of Public Education.

forts from the state, still do not cover the necessities occasioned by the integration of women into the work force. *For this reason we recommend that the appropriate agencies study the following propositions so that they might be applied in coming years:*

— To implement more arrangements for vacations and weekends, to extend boarding school schedules and other solutions which would contribute to improved care for children, the sick, and the elderly.

— To increase certain types of industrial and food services that would facilitate housework.

— To study the appropriateness of establishing nation-wide special hours for working women in shops selling food and manufactured articles, laundries, dry cleaners, appliance repair shops, etc.

— To study the business hours of commercial enterprises in order to establish, throughout the country, those which best fit the needs of working women.

— To review the operation of the pre-sale plan (the Jaba Plan) and of the CTC-MINCIN card, in order to introduce any changes suggested by experience and the present state of supplies.

— To increase and improve the quality of services rendered in laundries and dry cleaners, including self-service laundromats.

— To increase the availability of articles which would facilitate the housework of working families.

— To study the possibility of importing or producing nationally cloth containing synthetic fibers; this would alleviate the work of washing, drying, and ironing, especially in the case of clothing for school children.

— To control the sale of scarce domestic-use and personal-use manufactured articles so that these items may benefit working women, who, because of their work schedule, have little chance of acquiring them any other way.

— To study the possibility of bringing to the residence home-repair services (plumbing, electrical and carpentry work, masonry, and upholstering) which would alleviate the burden of housekeeping.

— To analyze the possibility of evening hours for gynecological and obstetrical clinics and to include pediatric services in this analysis as well.

— To increase, in work centers with appropriate conditions, nurseries for the children of working mothers. Such areas would permit vacation arrangements for the children of working women during extended and short school vacation periods and on Saturdays.

— To extend and improve the present vacation schedules organized in those schools with boarders.

— To disseminate more information on the benefits offered by special services created for the working woman, as well as on the hours these services are open to the public.

Care and Education of the Children.
Responsibility of the Father and the Mother

Clearly, even though significant resources have been invested, and will be invested, in these plans, they still do not satisfy the growing demand generated by a citizenry eager to participate in and offer their support to the revolution.

It is also imperative that men and women share responsibility for the care and education of the child. It is a pedagogical and psychological reality that boys and girls need both parents equally.

The concept that child care is the exclusive province of the mother should be rejected. The lovely responsibility of caring for children, watching over their studies, taking them to school, attending parents' meetings, meeting their friends, knowing their thoughts, guiding them in life, and teaching them revolutionary principles is a duty which both father and mother undertake equally.

When both parents have responsibilities in social production, the appropriate agencies must make opportunities available for father and mother alike to share the care of sick children, at home and in health care centers.

Attitude Concerning the Necessity of Integrating Women

All solutions which contribute to alleviating housework will facilitate a greater participation of men and women in economic, social, political, and cultural activities. *But present material limitations must not serve as an excuse not to attack problems which can be at least partially resolved. Diverse problems stem from the attitudes expressed by representatives of revolutionary power, at all state and political levels, toward the twofold necessity of integrating women into the work force and of retaining them in their positions.*

Unfortunately, not all representatives of revolutionary power demonstrate, in practice, such a consciousness; and, in order to develop it, a consistent ideological effort must be maintained. Such an effort should logically be directed by party militants and Young Communists in close coordination with state agencies and mass organizations.

Socialist Emulation. The Working Mother

Several matters deserve special attention; for example, encouraging working women in a dual social role, in particular working mothers, who care for their children while simultaneously contributing to society. Because they expend great efforts to carry out their labor responsibilities efficiently, they undoubtedly merit our entire nation's special recognition.

In addition, working mothers customarily perform all the domestic chores; as we have reiterated in this document, these chores are not yet shared in many homes. Nevertheless, specific expressions of incomprehension concerning the problems of these working women are manifested in their work centers. Such cases occur when similar demands are mechanically established for the working women who are mothers and for the rest of the workers, by applying the same evaluative criteria for both groups when analyzing justified absences (or volunteer work or study). In applying indices of socialist emulation, it is necessary to eradicate schematic criteria which fail to take into account the real difficulties which confront working women and which deny them the encouragement they deserve.

It is necessary to analyze the participation of women — particularly that of working mothers — in the socialist emulation by

*taking into account their problems, so that these difficulties do
not detract from either the woman or her work center.*

*Analysis of the Occupational Situation.
Training and Requalification*

At the present time, one of the circumstances seriously
hindering the incorporation of women into social work is the lack
of training of thousands of women willing to occupy available
positions.

To overcome such a situation, unemployed women must be
educated technically and culturally so that they attain conditions
of equality and occupy those labor positions which require certain
qualifications.

On the other hand, it is essential to study the possibility of
the working woman's self-improvement each day on the job so
that she may be in a position to assume greater responsibilities.

An analysis of the labor force shows that only 25.3 percent
are women. The occupational structure shows us the following:

TABLE I

Occupational Categories	Occupational Distribution by Sex		
	Total Percent	Percent Women	Percent Men
Laborers	100	11.6	88.4
Service Workers	100	48.7	51.3
Technicians	100	49.1	50.9
Administrative Personnel	100	67.5	32.5
Managers	100	15.3	84.7

TABLE II

Sector	Total	Men	Women	Percent Women
Light Industry	88.133	49,073	39,060	44.3
Cubatabaco	49,310	22,473	26,837	54.4
INIT [1]	79,177	46,823	32,354	40.9
MINSAP [2]	131,005	47,577	83,428	63.6
MINED [3]	224,694	91,864	132,830	59.1

TABLE III

Distribution of Working Women by Occupational Category

Sector	Total Percent	Percent Laborers	Percent Service Workers	Percent Technicians	Percent Administrative Personnel	Percent Managers
Light Industry	100	81	2	4	10	3
Cubatabaco	100	93	1	1	4	1
INIT [1]	100	23	65	2	6	4
MINSAP [2]	100	8	41	42	6	3
MINED [3]	100	4	22	65	5	4

[1] National Institute of Tourism.
[2] Ministry of Public Health.
[3] Ministry of Public Education.

Comparing Tables I and III, we could speculate that female participation is linked to training, since INIT, which does not require training, enrolls sixty-five percent women in services and twenty-three percent as laborers. And, in Table I, we see a low percentage of women in that sector of the labor force which generally demands skill requirements.

Now then, it must be emphasized that in MINSAP and in

MINED there is a high percentage of qualified personnel and that the greatest number of working women is found in these agencies.

What *is* evident is the low percentage of managers in all sectors, even in those employing many women; this demonstrates that we have not yet reached the goals proposed by the revolution — that women occupy their appropriate place, in accordance with their development and level.

Some Organizational Methods and Possible Forms of Employment Which Would Facilitate Working Women's Fulfillment of Their Duties

It is recommended that all appropriate agencies study and possibly implement the following measures:

— Organize special courses to retrain working women during times which permit the participation of *compañeras* otherwise unable to attend.

— Include the needs of the female sector in programs planned by labor organizations and control strictly the implementation of these programs. Establish courses for incorporating unemployed women in existing positions as well as in new ones which are planned.

— Establish part-time schedules which would facilitate women's employment in workdays of less than eight hours. These schedules should also be analyzed in order to ascertain if they could be applied to those women who, after childbirth, lack child care facilities and must give up working.

— Establish new forms of work: by contract, by the job, and even at home, in accordance with the requirements and possibilities of the economy.

— Establish free Saturdays, as long as the production and services in question permit this and as long as appropriate conditions exist in the centers. Present experience suggests that such action is advisable because the presence of children in the work centers constitutes a danger for them, hinders the work of the mothers and of the collectivity, and, therefore, proves detrimental to production or services.

— Organize the staff in accordance with the realistic necessities of centers where the majority of workers are women and modify it wherever necessary; since, as presently constituted, the staff cannot cope with the needs occasioned by maternity leaves, vacations, illness of the working woman or her family members, etc. This deficiency creates an overload for the other working women.

APPENDIX II: "I'LL COOK IF I HAVE TO"

A look at Cuba's youth indicates how far women in Cuba have developed since the revolution, and some of the issues to be resolved in the future. "I'll Cook If I Have To" is an article that appeared in the *Granma Weekly Review*, March 18, 1979. The article is quoted in its entirety:

> To find out what Cuba's youngest generation had to say about women in the revolution, we picked a school at random — the Jose Machado Primary School in Old Havana — and talked with the Pioneer Council there. The Council, elected by the students to run their affairs, was a typical one: the majority were girls. (Nation-wide some seventy percent of the Pioneer leadership is female). The conversation with these fifth and sixth graders was revealing, and reflected, at every turn, the clash between old and new values, between their parents' reality and the students' vision of themselves.
>
> *Here we have the best Pioneers, and they're almost all girls. Why is that?* SEVERAL TOGETHER: Girls lead better. . . . Girls are more organized. They're more disciplined. . . . Some are. There are boys that are disciplined and organized, too.
>
> *Do boys make good leaders?* ANDRES: Yes, I think boys can be demanding, and they know how to fulfill their responsibilities — but so do girls. When we went to a class for heads of school collectives in the municipality, there were only three boys, me and two others.
>
> *Will there always be more girl leaders or will that change?* ANDRES: I'm sure it will change!

What do you think? Don't you think Andrés is a bit male chauvinistic? EVERYONE: No!

What does male chauvinist mean? SARA: Not letting the girls develop, only the boys. . . . ISBET: Because there are men that want to be superior to women, that want to be better than women.

And should men do part of the housework? EVERYONE: Yes!

Who washes the dishes at your house? XIOMARA: I do. My mom and I do the cleaning. I have a brother in junior high schol and he goes to the store. . . . ANDRES: My dad helps out in the house when my grandmother is sick. And he's a sailor, so he's gone a few months at a time. . . . MARIA MERCEDES: My dad cleans. He helps out. But he doesn't cook. Sometimes he washes dishes — sometimes. . . . ANDRES: It isn't fair that if the woman works, the man doesn't help with the housework.

Do you know how to iron? ANDRES: I don't know how to iron pants and things, but I iron my scarf and I can iron shirts.

What do you all do after school? On weekends? EVERYONE: Go to the movies! MARIA MERCEDES: And the boys play baseball.

Why only the boys? MARIA MERCEDES: Because they need to develop their muscles (laughter).

And the girls? MARIA MERCEDES: Yes, but in other things. . . . MAGDALENA: I like volleyball, judo, and karate — and I like boxing!

What if a girl wanted to play ball with you? ANDRES: Well, we'd try to teach her.

What do girls play? ARACELYS: Jacks, hopscotch, parcheesi, and checkers.

And boys don't like that? PEDRO: Sure, we like parcheesi and checkers.

How many of your mothers work? (Hands of five out of eight go up.)

And what do they do? My mom's a secretary in the sugar industry.... Mine, too.... a factory worker.... school secretary ... works in the National Bank.

Are there things men can do better than women? EVERY-ONE: No! No!... ANDRES: There are women internationalists, like doctors, engineers, and teachers, who go to help other countries just like men....

Nothing then? ANDRES: Well, I guess they can play ball better (laughter).... MARIA MERCEDES: I think we need to form a team just to show Andrés that it's not just boys who know how to play baseball (Applause and laughter)!

Can women do some things better than men? ANDRES: Yes! Cook.... EVERYONE ELSE: No!... ANDRES: Well, they have more practice.

But why? Because men don't help cook? MARIA MER-CEDES: Not all men — my grandfather cooks. XIOMARA: My dad works at the Sevilla Hotel. He's a waiter and he knows how to do everything — and he cooks at home.... PEDRO: My dad knows how to cook eggs and rice (greeted by plenty of hooting).

Pedro, are you going to cook? Well, if I have to. I guess if my wife isn't home, I'll have to cook.

Have you thought about what you want to be when you grow up? EVERYONE: Sure! A diplomat, an ambassador ... a member of the Communist Party and a doctor ... a pediatrician ... a chemist ... a performer ... an engineer ... a doctor ... an engineer....

So, we'll have to come back in a few years to see which of these aspirations have been fulfilled — and which Pioneers are doing the cooking!

APPENDIX III:
THE WORKING WOMAN MATERNITY LAW *

FOREWORD

Protection of maternity and childhood by the state was a principle formally proclaimed in Cuba by the more progressive bourgeois law. However, the scarce and irregular social and economic development of our country, plus the vices that characterized the period of the pseudorepublic, not only limited but also largely sidetracked that much-touted protection.

Maternity Leave was established in Cuba in 1934, supposedly to benefit all working mothers-to-be. However, it never met the needs of the great majority of these women, since its benefits were not extended to either farm women or to the vast army of maids and other women who did odd jobs, so typical of that society.

The Revolution always proclaimed the intention, in keeping with its principles, of putting into effect the protection and care of the working people masses. Along with other measures following the triumph of the Revolution in January 1959, Cuba began to develop the material foundations for providing preventive medical care and hospitalization to women and children and to the people in general. One of the outstanding achievements in this direction was the rapid extension of these services to the most remote areas of the country.

Law 1100 of March 27, 1963, generalized Social Security in our country and included the following concerning maternity leave:

a) extended the benefits to all working mothers-to-be in both state anl private sectors;

b) guaranteed a 12-week pre- and post-natal paid leave of absence;

c) granted every working mother one hour a day, within

* Law No. 1263 of January 14, 1974, published in the Official Gazette of January 16, 1974, available in English from the Ministry of Justice.

her regular working hours, for breast-feeding and caring for her baby;

d) *provided whatever services and material kinds the mother-to-be and her baby might need during her pregnancy and until mother and child are sent home from the maternity hospital; and*

e) *granted a subsidy in cash to working mothers who gave birth without making use of state hospitals.*

Moreover, the broad and accelerated general development of the country attained by the Revolution, especially in the field of public health, made it possible that on January 16, 1974, law 1263, on working women's maternity, be enacted.

The draft was drawn up by a special commision composed of representatives of the Ministry of Labor, the Ministry of Public Health, the Central Organization of Cuban Trade Unions, the Federation of Cuban Women, the Children's Daycare Centers, the Children's Institute and the Ministry of Education. A number of changes were made and the draft enriched by the suggestions made by working women when it was discussed and analyzed by the people.

Among other things, Law 1263:

a) *increases the benefits of maternity leave, in recognition of women's contributions to the construction of socialist society;*

b) *guarantees medical care during pregnancy, at birth and during the post-natal period;*

c) *guarantees medical care for the mother and the newborn child;*

d) *extends the period of paid maternity leave to 18 weeks, 12 of them after birth. In case of multiple pregnancy or errors in predicting the date of birth, this period is extended another two weeks; and*

e) *guarantees an additional non-paid leave of absence for those mothers who cannot go to work because they have to stay at home to take care of their children.*

This Law is an example of the level of development reached

*by our country in the field of public health and affirms how the
rights proclaimed in this field have been put into effect.*

*This booklet includes the full text of Law 1263 and its reg-
ulations.*

EXECUTIVE BRANCH

COUNCIL OF MINISTERS

I, OSVALDO DORTICOS TORRADO, *President of the
Republic of Cuba,*

HEREBY PROCLAIM: That the Council of Ministers has
approved and I have signed the following:

WHEREAS: Studies made on problems pertaining to working women, especially those relating to maternity, counsel the
enactment of new legislation in order to grant the maximum guarantee to all maternity rights which, although recognized and
provided for by Social Security Law No. 1100 of March 27, 1963,
should be reconsidered on the basis of present-day medical and
scientific principles.

WHEREAS: It is a primary interest of the Revolutionary
Government to give special attention to the working mother
since, in addition to her valuable contribution to society in the
procreation and education of children, she also fulfills her social
duty by working.

WHEREAS: A successful pregnancy as well as the delivery
and the future health of the child require the adoption of adequate measures on the part of the pregnant woman, as an ineluct-
able duty toward her child and society.

WHEREAS: To secure the above-mentioned measures, it is
necessary to ensure medical attention and rest to the working
woman during her pregnancy, the breastfeeding of the newborn
during the first months of life which will protect him from
disease and favor the development of strong emotional bonds
between mother and child, and the systematic medical examination of the child by a pediatrician during his first year of life.

WHEREAS: In our country all medical and hospital services, including pharmaceutical and hospital dietary services related to maternity are guaranteed free of charge to all the population. This makes it necessary to establish additional legislation on the enjoyment of said rights by the working woman or the wife or the companion of a worker.

THEREFORE: By virtue of the authority vested on them, the Council of Ministers resolves to dictate the following:

LAW No. 1263

WORKING WOMAN MATERITY LAW

CHAPTER I

Scope and Protection

Article 1. The present Law comprises the working woman and protects her maternity, guaranteeing and facilitating, in a special manner, her medical attention during pregnancy, her rest before and after delivery, the breastfeeding and care of the children as well as a financial aid in those cases specified in these provisions.

CHAPTER II

Paid Leave

Article 2. Every pregnant working woman, regardless of type of work will be obliged to stop working on the 34th week of pregnancy, and will have the right to a leave of absence of 18 weeks, which will include 6 weeks before delivery and 12 weeks after delivery. This leave will be paid as determined by this Law, provided that the working woman meets the requirements stated in Article 11.

The Ministry of Labour, at the proposal of the Central Organization of Cuban Trade Unions, will regulate exceptional situations in those places of work whose special characteristics, according to medical and scientific criteria, make it necessary that working women take prenatal leave for longer periods than those established by this Law.

Article 3. In cases of multiple pregnancy, the working woman will be obliged to stop working on the 32nd week of pregnancy, extending to eight weeks the period of her paid leave before delivery.

Article 4. If delivery does not take place during the period established for the prenatal leave, this leave will be extended to the date on which delivery takes place and the extended time period will be paid for up to two weeks.

Article 5. If delivery takes place before the expiry of the prenatal leave, this leave will cease and the working woman will begin her postnatal leave.

Article 6. If delivery takes place before the 34th week of pregnancy, or before the 32nd week in the case of multiple pregnancy, the leave will include only the postnatal period.

Article 7. The working woman will be guaranteed a postnatal leave of six weeks necessary for her recovery even when because of adverse circumstances of accident or acquired or congenital diseases, the child dies at birth or during the first four weeks after birth.

Article 8. If the working woman, because of complications during delivery, requires a longer period of recovery beyond the postnatal leave, she will have the right to receive the subsidy for illness as established in the Social Security Law.

CHAPTER III

Accidents of Pregnancy

Article 9. Accidents of pregnancy are those complications relative to pregnancy or diseases acquired during pregnancy which require absolute bed rest by doctor's order, with or without hospitalization.

Accidents of pregnancy which occur before the 34th week will give the working woman the right to subsidy for illness as established in the Social Security Law.

Chapter IV

Financial Aid

Article 10. The financial aid that the working woman will receive during her maternity leave will be equal to the weekly average of salaries and subsidies she has received during the twelve months immediately prior to the leave. This aid will never be under ten pesos a week.

Article 11. In order to have the right to receive the paid maternity leave established by this Law, it will be indispensable that the working woman has an expedient in due form, exception made in the case of administrative negligence, and worked not less than 75 days in the twelve months immediately prior to the leave. However, even when the working woman does not fulfill these requirements, she will have the right to receive the complementary leaves established in the following chapter.

Chapter V

Complementary Maternity Leave

Article 12. During pregnancy and up to the 34th week, the working woman will have the right to six days or twelve halfdays of paid leave for her medical and dental care prior to delivery.

Article 13. In order to guarantee the care and development of the child during his first year of life, the working women will have the right every month to one day off, with pay, to take her child for a pediatric check-up.

CHAPTER VI

Unpaid Leave

Article 14. The working mother will have the right to an unpaid leave for the purpose of taking care of her children, under the terms and conditions established by this Law.

INTERIM PROVISIONS

FIRST: The present Law will be applied to all working women who, at the time of its promulgation, have fulfilled 34 weeks of pregnancy and have still not taken their maternity leave, and to those who are already on leave according to Social Security Law No. 1100 of March 27, 1963, as regards the extension of the leave to twelve weeks after delivery and one day off, with pay, every month for pediatric visits. Additional payment to cover the extended postnatal leave will be given as established in this Law.

SECOND: The extra hour of rest period that for child care established Law No. 1100 of March 27, 1963 [sic], will remain for those working women now enjoying this benefit.

THIRD: The women worker [sic] enjoying unpaid leave, as established in Instruction No. 1 of the Labour Justice Office of the Ministry of Labour, dated September 23, 1968, will maintain the same labour rights established in said Instruction, until the expiry of their [sic] leave.

FINAL PROVISIONS

FIRST: The Ministry of Labour is authorized to dictate as many provisions as required for the execution and application of this Law.

SECOND: Title II of Law No. 1100 of March 27, 1963, Instruction No. 1 of the Labour Justice Office of the Ministry of Labour dated September 23, 1968, and all other provisions and rulings which oppose the fulfillment of this Law, are hereby abrogated. This Law will go into effect on the date of its promulgation in the Official Gazette of the Republic.

THEREFORE: I command that this Law be fulfilled and enforced in all its parts.

SIGNED, at the Palace of the Revolution, in Havana, on January 14th, 1974.

OSVALDO DORTICOS TORRADO

Fidel Castro Ruz
Prime Minister

Oscar Fernández Padilla
Minister of Labour

APPENDIX IV: REGULATIONS OF LAW 1263 *

MINISTRY OF LABOUR

RESOLUTION No. 2

WHEREAS: Law No. 1263 of January 14, 1974, in the First Final Provisions authorizes the passing of as many provisions as required for the execution and enforcement of said Law.

THEREFORE: By virtue of the authority vested in me,

I Resolve:

FIRST: To dictate for the execution and enforcement of Law No. 1263 of January 14, 1974, the following:

---

* Resolution No. 2 of the Minister of Labor of January 15, 1974, published in the *Official Gazette* of January 16, 1974, and available in English from the Ministry of Justice.

REGULATIONS

Responsibility of the Administration
in Working Centers

Article 1. The Administration in all working centers will be responsible for payments of all financial aid stipulated in Law No. 1263 of January 14, 1974.

Article 2. The Administration will have the obligation of granting maternity leave after the 34th week of pregnancy — or after the 32nd week of pregnancy in case of multiple births — once the working woman presents the medical certificate required.

Article 3. The fulfillment of the paid leave stipulated in Article 2 and 7 of the Law will take place in three parts: The first, at the beginning of the prenatal leave; the second, at the beginning of the first six weeks of the postnatal leave; and the third, at the beginning of the last six weeks of the postnatal leave, when applicable.

Article 4. In exceptional cases when delivery does not take place within the six-week period of the prenatal leave, the said leave will be extended until delivery actually takes place; payment for the additional period will never be over a term of two weeks, after which it will be considered an unpaid leave.

Article 5. The payment of the two weeks stipulated in the preceding Article, will be made jointly with the payment of the six weeks of the postnatal leave.

Article 6. If delivery takes place before the expiry of the prenatal leave, the financial difference between this date and the original expiry of the leave will be deducted from the postnatal leave, as stipulated in Article 5 of the Law.

Article 7. In order to grant the rights stipulate [sic] by the Law, the Administration will be responsible in all cases to demand the medical certificates or assistance notes to medical services issued by establishments of the Ministry of Public Health.

Article 8. The Administration will have the obligation to guarantee that the working woman who reassumes her work upon expiry of the maternity leave will have the right to occupy the same post she had before.

The Amount of Payment

Article 9. In order to calculate the average weekly income, referred in Article 10 of the Law, the salaries and subsidies received by the working woman during the twelve months immediately prior to the start of the maternity leave, will be added up and its result divided by 52 weeks.

Article 10. The procedure to calculate the amount of payment established in the previous Article will be applied in all cases, including those working women with a work record of less than one year. Trial periods in the case of new workers will be included for the purpose of calculation.

Article 11. A temporary working woman with a work record will have the right to a paid maternity leave and receive the payment even when the start of the same does not coincide with her cycle of work. The amount of payment will be calculated in the same way as for other working women.

Article 12. The right to paid leave will be granted to the pregnant woman with 75 or more work-days, from the time when she should have been properly accredited as a worker even though she was not because of administrative negligence.

Article 13. Working women who have not worked during the period established in Article 11 of the Law, will have the right to pre- and postnatal leaves, without payment, as established by the Law. However, all other complementary leaves will be paid.

Unpaid Leave

Article 14. If the working woman cannot work because she must take care of her children, she will have the right to an unpaid leave of up to:

a) nine months, if the leave starts with the expiry of the postnatal leave or any time after it. This leave will expire when the child is one year old;

b) six months for all working mothers with children under 16 years of age.

Article 15. Rights previously established will be granted initially for a maximum period of three months, renewable every three months if the original motive for the leave is still valid.

Article 16. If a working woman returns to work according to the terms established for the unpaid leave, she will have the right to occupy her former post.

Article 17. The Administration, after hearing the opinion of the Trade-Union Local, may extend the leave when exceptional circumstances so advise, but in no case may the extension be for more than three months after the expiry of the terms established in Article 14. After this period of time, or after the extension if such is the case, the working woman will be separated and her post occupied, following the existing evaluation norms.

Article 18. In order to receive the leave regulated by paragraph b) of Article 14 of this Regulations [sic], it will be indispensable that the working woman may have been hired by a working center and have actually worked two thirds of the workdays of the semester prior to the date of the request for leave.

In cases of new workers the trial periods will be included for the calculation of payments.

Article 19. Unpaid leave may be granted in short periods, of not less than one week, and will be accumulative until the maximum time period established is reached. If between one leave and another, the working woman works uninterruptedly for a period similar to the one established in the previous Article, she will have the right to a new leave.

SECOND: All provisions which are contrary to the dispositions of the present Regulations are hereby abrogated. These provisions will become effective on the date of its [sic] publication in the Official Gazette of the Republic.

SIGNED, In Havana, Ministry of Labour on the 15th day of January, 1974.

OSCAR FERNANDEZ PADILLA
Minister of Labour

Bibliography

Agüero, Dra. Nisia. *La urbanización rural en Cuba.* Havana: Editorial de Ciencias Sociales, Instituto del Libro, 1975.

Cassa, Roberto. *Los Tainos de la Española.* Santo Domingo, Dominican Republic: Editora de la Universidad de Santo Domingo, 1974.

Céspedes, Francisco Garzón. *Un teatro de sus protagonistas.* Havana: UNEAC, 1977.

Cuban Public Health Ministry work team. *La atención materno infantil y la reducción de la mortalidad perinatal en Cuba.* Prepared for the XXX Anniversary Congress of the Mexican Social Security Institute, January 1974.

del Olmo, Dr. Humberto Sinobas. *VIII Congreso Latinoamericaño de obstetricia y ginecología: 17 años de ginecología, obstetricia y neonatología.* Havana, 1976.

de la Riva, Juan Pérez. "Presentación de un censo ignorado: el padrón general de 1778," *Revista de la Biblioteca Nacional Jose Marti.* Havana, 1977.

de la Torre, Silvio. *Mujer y sociedad.* Santa Clara: Universidad Central de las Villas, 1965.

Deschamps, Pedro. *El negro en la economía habera del siglo XIX.* Havana: UNEAC, 1971.

Editorial de Ciencias Sociales. *Los asentamientos humanos en Cuba.* Havana: Instituto del Libro, 1975.

Editorial Orbe. *Memorias: II Congreso Nacional de la Federación de Mujeres Cubanas.* Havana: 1975. (Thesis and Resolution on the role of the family in socialism.)

Engels, Frederick. *The Origin of the Family, Private Property and the State.* New York: International Publishers, 1942.

Guerra, Ramiro. *Manual de historia de Cuba.* Havana: Ciencias Sociales, Ministerio de Cultura, 1971.

Huberman Leo and Paul Sweezy. *Socialism in Cuba.* New York: Monthly Review Press, 1962.

Lenin on the Emancipation of Women. Moscow: Progress Publishers, 1968.

Mass, Bonnie. *The Population Target.* Toronto: Canadian Women's Educational Press, 1975.

Martínez-Alier, Verena. "El honor de la mujer en Cuba en el siglo XIX," *Revista de la Biblioteca Nacional José Martí.* Havana, 1970.

_____. *Marriage, Class and Colour in Nineteenth-Century Cuba: A Study of Racial Attitudes and Sexual Values in a Slave Society.* Cambridge: Cambridge University Press, 1974.

McDonald, Marian. "Radical Forum" on the abortion question in *The Guardian,* 1978.

Ministerio de Cultura. *Las estadísticas demográficas cubanas.* Havana: Ciencias Sociales, 1975.

_____. *La población de Cuba.* Havana: Centros de Estudios Demográficos, Ciencias Sociales, 1976.

_____. *20 años de matrimonios en Cuba.* Havana: Ciencias Sociales, 1977.

Ministerio de Justicia. *Working Woman's Maternity Law.* Havana, 1975.

_____. *La mujer en Cuba socialista.* Havana: Editorial Orbe, 1977. Contains the Family Code, Thesis Three, the Constitution, and the Maternity Law.

Ortíz, Fernando. *Los negros esclavos.* Havana: Ministerio de Cultura, Ciencias Sociales, 1975.

Poumier, Maria. *Apuntes sobre la vida cotidiana en Cuba en 1898.* Havana: Ministerio de Cultura, Ciencias Sociales, 1975.

Primer Congreso del Partido Comunista de Cuba. *Tesis y Resoluciones.* Havana: Departamento de Orientación Revolucionaria del Comité Central del Partido Comunista de Cuba, 1976.

Randall, Margaret. *Cuban Women Now.* Toronto: The Women's Press, 1974.

_____. *La mujer cubana ahora.* Havana: Ciencias Sociales, 1972.

_____. *La situación de la mujer.* Lima, Peru: Ediciones Centro, Centro de Estudios de Participación Popular, 1974.

_____. "You can't make a revolution without them." Toronto: LAWG and Canadian Women's Educational Press, 1975.

_____. *Sueños y Realidades del Guajiricantor*. Mexico City: Siglo XXI, 1979.

_____. Conversations with Dra. Nisia Agüero of Grupo de Desarrollo de Comunidades. Havana, 1978.

_____. Interviews with Dr. Enso Dueñas, Acting Director of the Ramón González Coro Maternity Hospital, and Dra. Isabel Delfino, head of Psychology at the same hospital. Havana, 1978.

Regalado, Antero. *Las luchas campesinas en Cuba*. Havana: Departamento de Orientación Revolucionaria del Comité Central del Partido Comunista de Cuba, 1974.

Sejourné, Laurette. *Teatro Escambray: una experiencia*. Havana: Editorial de Ciencias Sociales, 1977.

Tabío, E. and E. Rey. *Prehistoria de Cuba*. Havana: Academia de Ciencias de Cuba, 1966.

U.S.-C.H.E. Newsletter, Spring 1975.